STILL TIME
for
ETERNITY

Published by
The Bible Reading Fellowship
First Floor, Elsfield Hall
15–17 Elsfield Way,
Oxford OX2 8FG
ISBN 1 84101 212 2

First published 2001
10 9 8 7 6 5 4 3 2 1 0

Acknowledgments
Scripture quotations are taken from The New Revised Standard Version of the Bible,
Anglicized Edition, copyright © 1989, 1995 by the Division of Christian Education of
the National Council of the Churches of Christ in the USA, and are used by
permission. All rights reserved.

A catalogue record for this book is available from the British Library

Printed and bound in Great Britain by Omnia Books Limited, Glasgow

STILL TIME
for
ETERNITY

Margaret
CUNDIFF

For Peter, Julian and Alison, my great support team,
with love and thanks.

CONTENTS

Introduction: A new day dawning   7

1   By hand   11

2   Castaway or new way?   16

3   'The end is nigh'—or is it?   20

4   Written in the book   24

5   The thinking angel   29

6   Man of the people—man of God   33

7   Why are you afraid?   38

8   Not too big to say sorry   42

9   Whose child is it?   46

10   City of God   51

11   But what if...?   56

12   An outward and visible sign   60

13   Come fly with me   64

14   Take your shoes off   69

15   Man of sorrows   74

16   Cross, not clock   78

17   On the eighth day   82

18   Come and see   87

19   Who am I?   92

20   The joy that knows no ending   97

21   What sort of a God?   101

22	Just a second	105
23	All one family	109
24	Treasure seekers	113
25	Falling leaves	118
26	Out of the flood	122
27	Spot the differences	126
28	The missing link	130
29	Called to account	134
30	Just ten minutes	138
31	All change	143
32	Beginning again	147
33	Heavens above	152
34	Is there still time?	156

A NEW DAY DAWNING

I was first consciously made aware of the coming of the new millennium at the beginning of the 1950s. I was a student, still just able to call myself a teenager, fired with evangelical fervour. I was training for 'full-time work in the Church'—although I had only a vague understanding of what that might mean—and was finding life in a theological college in Oxford a real cultural shock, having up to that point lived in a small northern town. After leaving school at fourteen, and in the five years since then working in a wide variety of humdrum jobs, ranging from apprentice cook, painter, to junior typist and wages clerk, life as a student was definitely different and I was determined to make the most of it, to discover for myself the possibilities that were all around me.

At a Saturday night meeting of students I remember the speaker saying, 'We are now in the final half century before the new millennium, time is short—what are you going to do?' Fifty years! I hadn't much clue about the next twelve months, never mind fifty years. Anyway, in fifty years' time would I still be alive? I very much doubted whether I would, so what could I have to say or do about any millennium?

So I promptly forgot about it! That is, until the late 1980s when I went to a meeting in York about the Decade of Evangelism. The speaker challenged us, as Christian ministers and leaders, to have a sense of urgency: 'Time is short, what are you going to do?' 'I have heard this before!' I thought. The speaker outlined various possibilities for action, and again urged us to get on with it saying, 'Ten years may seem a long time now, but I guarantee if I come back here in ten years time, just before the clock strikes midnight on 31 December 1999, some of you will still be thinking about it!'

How true his words proved to be! From then on, though there

were constant murmurings about the imminent decade and millennium, committees were formed, conferences held, papers written, and some feverish activity took place, with varying degrees of success.

During the last year or so of the decade and millennium, people generally began to be stirred, taking an interest in the progress of the Millennium Dome, arguing about what would be in it and, more to the point, who would pay for it. Plans were made to celebrate the millennium, fears were expressed, the dreaded term 'millennium bug' was on everyone's lips; governments, firms and institutions began to panic, and then to issue statements that everything was completely under control, well, almost under control, as far as could be seen... Rumblings were heard from various religious groups as to the very real possibility that Jesus Christ would return on the stroke of midnight, and an Internet link was offered so Christians could actually watch the Messiah's return through the Golden Gate—the Eastern Gate—in Jerusalem.

In June 1999 something happened that stopped in its tracks the frenetic dash to the millennium—the death of Cardinal Basil Hume. Some weeks before his death he had written of his terminal cancer, that he would not be on this earth much longer, and he wrote simply and movingly of his Christian faith which had sustained him throughout his life, and which he was sure would continue to sustain him through the last part of his journey into eternity. When the news of his death came it was almost as though the whole country came to a standstill, mourning the loss of a man who had been such an example of holiness and faith. People of all faiths and none felt they had lost a friend and guide.

We stopped, we pondered, we grieved; we had been given the chance to hear the 'still small voice', time to listen, to be, before we plunged back into the headlong rush towards the millennium. For some it was a life-changing experience, for others just a day or two to reflect and adjust. Seeds of hope were sown, which were not of human manufacture, but the gift of God through the life and death of a holy man.

The possibility of the end of the world on 4 July was greeted by what might be described as 'amused trepidation'. Not many took very seriously the prophecy of the sixteenth-century physician and astrologer Nostradamus, even though endless column inches and radio and television time were devoted to him and his prophecies—majoring on the one which would seem to predict the end of the world on 4 July 1999—later amended to possibly August... next February... The day of Nostradamus came and went, people heaved a sigh of relief and life went back to normal—whatever normal might be.

But then another date loomed up, 11 August, the date of the full solar eclipse, the first since 1927. The media were full of stories of what might occur. Cornwall had standing-room only, and rumours flew around of the overcharging of tourists intent on seeing the eclipse from the best possible vantage point. There were warnings about eye damage, and gloomy weather forecasts—if the day was overcast, nothing would be seen at all. The predictions ranged from complete darkness and chaos, to a gentle glow. As the date grew nearer, again there was a sense of uncertainty—what would happen, was it a 'sign of the times', an omen even of what might be? It came, it happened, we waited and then the sun again appeared in its full glory. We revelled in its light and heat and breathed a sigh of relief and got on with our lives.

Autumn came, then the quickening pace of winter, the 'Christmas rush' but this time with a blurring of the edges of Christmas and millennium, a jumble of preparations, announcements, warnings, and still that 'millennium bug' hovered over us all. Fact or fiction—who could tell—but we were to take no chances, and prepare ourselves for what might be. Christmas came and went, we all eased ourselves out of the Christmas spirit into the millennium celebrations. For some it involved a frenzy of activity, for the rest, watching it on television. For 24 hours, as dawn broke around the world, the celebrations got under way, the Dome was open—just—although the London Eye, the great wheel, turned passengerless as it had failed its safety check.

Beacons blazed, fireworks exploded, people cheered and embraced, and our Queen joined hands with her subjects in singing 'Auld Lang Syne' as the seconds of 1999 ticked away into 2000. We had made it into the 21st century. It is all history now. We settled down again after all the hype and expectations, the hiccups and hopes. Time moved on, taking us with it, and whether we thought the millennium really began in 2000 or 2001, it has happened.

Yet the memories, the experiences of living through a particular period of time can provide us not only with something to look back on, but give us an incentive to go forward. During the winding up of the 20th century and the beginning of the 21st, there have been times when it has seemed that the world in general, and my own personal world, have stood still for a few moments, long enough to give time to see the bigger picture, the larger world, the working out of God's kingdom here on earth in the context of eternity. It is like a series of photographs which enable us to relive certain moments, reflect on them and, by taking a closer look, see if there is more to them than met our eye or took our attention when we looked through the viewfinder and pressed the button. This book is a series of such snapshots, set in the frame of God's word. I realize that other people's holiday snaps can be boring, but I hope you will enjoy sharing some of my stills of a very special period in history, and that they will encourage you to take a fresh look at some of your own, and share them with others—moments of time, captured in the heart, worth a second look before we all dash on. After all, there is still time for eternity, and isn't that what really matters?

Chapter 1

BY HAND

Sorting out—or trying to create more space in my very overcrowded desk—I came to a sudden stop in the proceedings when I unearthed a red leather autograph book belonging to 'Margaret Smith, aged twelve'. It had been a long time since I had looked at it, and it had found its way into the far recesses of a drawer. Now all my sorting out plans were abandoned as I gave myself to going down the pathways of the 1940s contained in that book.

The book had been a Christmas present from my parents—Christmas 1944. Collecting autographs was all the rage then, I remember, and everybody I knew had a special book. None of these pieces of paper, footballs and programmes—we serious autograph collectors provided a worthy vehicle to contain our treasured trophies, leather-backed books being the *crème de la crème*, and a red one, in my opinion anyway, being so attractive as to make those asked to write in it grateful for the honour bestowed upon them.

The first entry, in a strong, clear, even script read, 'Dear friend Peggy. My special greetings for Christmas 1944 are sent to you by a grateful American soldier. I will always remember your part in making my stay in England pleasant. Sincerely, Ed Hess. December 1944'. Some pages later, another entry from another American soldier: '16 April 1945. Dear Peg, On a swell furlough. Thanx. Love Fred.' Ed and Fred, twin brothers, young Americans from Maryland, stationed in Cheshire before going to France, invited to share our home by the said Peggy— my nickname—because I felt sorry for them being away from home.

My mother and I had met Fred and his friend Dick in a chip shop queue in Congleton, and given them some advice about their purchases, fish and chips being a new experience for the young American soldiers. We had struck up a conversation with them, during which they had asked us whether we knew of 'some church or YMCA where we could go to write our letters. Our parents have told us not to get in any trouble, but to go to a church and be among good folk'. My response was, 'You can come to our house!' At which Fred said, 'If that's an invitation, ma'am, we'd sure like to take it.' My mother confessed later she had felt a little uneasy. After all, what would my father say when two American soldiers turned up on our doorstep, invited by his twelve-year-old daughter? In the event my father was delighted, as his brother Peter serving in the Navy, had been made so welcome by an American family. When Fred's brother Ed also came to England he too found his way to our home, spending his first Christmas away from home 'at home' with us.

'Our Americans' all went to fight in France. Fred and Ed survived, although Fred was badly wounded, but sadly Fred's friend Dick was killed on his first day in action. The friendship between our families continued through the years, with Dick's family until the death of his parents, and with Fred until his death, and since then with his children and grandchildren. Ed, of the autograph book's front page, still writes to us in that same steady clear hand. We are one family, continuing through the generations, and will remain so, I am sure.

Every page of my autograph book brings back so many memories. I can see each person through their handwriting, the words they have written expressing their character too. My parents, teachers, friends, strangers, even some 'famous' people made their entry into my red leather book. As I look at their entries it is just as it was when they wrote them—such is the power of handwriting, their personality alive and present. I do not regret the time spent turning the pages slowly, savouring those entries, with all thoughts of 'sorting out' abandoned, and I promise to do it more often.

The same is true, perhaps more so, when from time to time I come across a pile of letters, in that file marked 'Letters. Save.' They are in no particular order, either of time or subject, and certainly in no alphabetical order. As the file says, they are letters I wanted to save.

Why? Again there are letters from my mother on various occasions, the last one written just days before her death. Her usually strong hand was a little shaky, the words uneven, but the love, courage and faith shine like beacons from the page. Then there are the letters from a spiritual adviser, his words of wisdom serving to remind me that truth stands eternal, that truth is built upon the word of God, honed by experience. Shared secrets and sadnesses, the opening of hearts, perhaps words that could not have been said face to face but only through a letter. And I hope that writing it all down would have felt like a release of those deep feelings and emotions into the safe keeping and understanding of a friend. As I appreciate the treasures that I have in that pile of letters, and the ones that constantly join them, I feel rather guilty as I look at my own handwriting, perhaps more of a scrawl than a work of art. Yet I take comfort from friends who tell me they treasure my letters, and what the words, however written, contain for them.

Sadly, handwriting letters seems to be going out of fashion. First, the telephone made communication of a very different kind easily accessible. Today, with e-mail, voice mail, fax and all the rest, who needs to take up a pen and paper? I confess that often I type my letters, for speed and legibility, and we do send a 'round robin' at Christmas time with family news, but I still cling doggedly to writing those very personal letters, in which I want to share at the deepest point with others, for I know from my own experience what a familiar handwriting means and conveys.

I do not claim to be an academic or historian but I am always excited and thrilled to see pieces of parchment containing writings preserved from thousands of years ago—the fragments of scripture, the letters from generations long gone, the descriptions of their lives and times, hopes and struggles. Seeing their writing, their signatures even, brings them to life for me, connects us through the power of pen and ink.

As I read the Bible, and I have so many different versions and trans-lations, I sometimes long to know for sure which is the truly authentic voice. Bible study groups can sometimes prove to be a minefield, when there may be as many different versions being read as members of the group; and I hesitate to say, 'You will use this one because then we will all be the same.' Minefield it may be, as we pick our way through, but it often proves to be a treasure store too, as we have the advantage of so much at our disposal to help us understand what is written from different points of view.

What if the words of Jesus were written in his hand for us to see, or the letters of Paul set out before us? How much difference would it make to our understanding? A thought to ponder! Much though the idea intrigues and excites me, I know I do not need that extra dimension, for the word of God is alive, active and personal. It leaps off the pages, speaks to the heart, provides strength, comfort, hope. It challenges, and yes, rebukes. It touches the soul in a way that not even the most precious form of human communication or correspondence can. As we step further into this new millennium with all its new ways of communication, the word of God will still achieve its purpose, for it is timeless and eternal, the living way for all people of every generation.

Indeed, the word of God is living and active, sharper than any two edged sword, piercing until it divides soul from spirit, joints from marrow; it is able to judge the thoughts and intentions of the heart. And before him no creature is hidden, but all are naked and laid bare to the eyes of the one to whom we must render an account.
HEBREWS 4:12–13

Father, thank you for the joy and power of the written word, the gift bestowed through writing. For the means of communication living on through stone, parchment, paper. Preserved through the ages, transferred in seconds by the means of modern technology, touching, holding, being, from heart to hand and back to heart again.

Thank you that you are our Living Word, revealed through the sacred writings, the work of your prophets, priests and kings. Thank you for the story of your people from the beginning of creation, and of your dealings with them. For 'the word made flesh' in Jesus, revealed to us by the anointing power of your Holy Spirit. For those who through writing interpreted your word,

proclaimed it, living by it, dying for it, so that we might enter into the joy of
it, receiving it into our hearts and lives. Thank you for your words of life,
entrusted to us to continue to share afresh in our generation, that others who
come after may read and know and spread the news of your power and love.

I will put my law within them, and I will write it on their hearts; and
I will be their God, and they shall be my people.
JEREMIAH 31:33

Chapter 2

CASTAWAY OR
NEW WAY?

The hymn writer Isaac Watts, at the beginning of the 18th century, described time as 'an ever-rolling stream', which brings into my mind a picture drawn from the Yorkshire Dales. I can see clear, sparkling water, meandering its way through the dales, providing refreshment, pleasure, activity, freedom. I can feel the sensual enjoyment of that water washing over my feet on a blistering hot day, the sense of awe watching the swollen stream gushing along after the winter's snow or rain, or exploring its almost stationary trickle in the height of a dry summer. To be carried along with it and in it, joining together with others from different places on our way to our final destination, seems very attractive.

But how would Isaac Watts describe time at the beginning of the 21st cemtury, I wonder? For most of us living today I suspect it feels more like being on an express train, travelling at ever-increasing speed, rocking to and fro, in imminent danger of getting madly out of control and finishing up as a disaster, which we passengers can do nothing about. How we long for that 'ever-rolling stream' rather than the back of a man-made monster.

Now and again voices of protest are heard, longing for a return to an earlier, quieter, more constructive form of living and thinking. 'Back to basics'; 'the good life'; 'the good old days'—a nostalgia for the past, the wish to switch life from 'fast forward' to 'reverse'. People want to be more creative, community-minded, harmonious—if it were ever so in the past, viewed through our rose-coloured 'shades'. The BBC thought that the year 2000 would be a good time to try such an experiment, and called for volunteers to spend the year marooned on a remote Scottish island, having to survive on basics, sharing a common life and building up a new-style community. Thousands of people from all walks of life and of all ages responded to the invitation. Numbers were whittled down to a short list and the survivors put through a gruelling practical exercise to decide which of them would actually be invited to become part of what was known as 'Castaway 2000'. I watched with a mixture of admiration, horror and increasing pessimism about such a project succeeding as I saw the programmes about the candidates, the testing of their suitability, and the beginning of the project. It seemed to have no common purpose except to make a television series, and to make a community for a social experiment rather than enriching the life of society today.

A few days ago I was with another community, not on a remote Scottish island, but in my beloved Yorkshire Dales, at Scargill House near Kettlewell. Scargill is a retreat, holiday and conference centre run by a community of mainly young people who come from all over the world as well as this country, because they believe it is where God wants them to be to serve him and others. While it is a haven of peace and prayer, it is also a busy, well-organized concern. Cleaning, cooking, keeping the estate in good condition, welcoming guests, running a busy office, are as much part of the life of community as prayer and worship, study and reflection. Exploring the Dales with a school party or delving deep into the scriptures with a group from a city parish is all part of that commitment to God and people, lived out humbly and joyfully, putting the concerns of others first—not to prove a point, but to follow in the footsteps of Jesus, living his way of life. It's not easy— people are people, not saints—but they draw strength from God and from their common life to do it. Scargill House is not unique, as in fact there are many such communities to be found in cities as well as in the countryside. Religious communities of monks and nuns have existed for many hundreds of years, opening their doors to all who want to discover more of God; who want to know how to live his way in a world which seems to have thrown out the rules which have been given to enable us to live as one world, one family, one community, rooted and grounded in God.

Jesus did not work in isolation, but called others to share with him. Those who responded to his call found themselves in a community of his followers. A strange group they were, with different backgrounds and temperaments, of different ages, abilities and expectations. They argued, were resentful, and at times exploded. They tried to jockey for position, were often ungracious and lacking in courtesy, but as they lived with Jesus and with each other they began to learn a new way of living and of serving. By the example of his love, and the power of his Spirit, they were changed and enabled to go out into the world fired by what he had done for them and in them. It is that same love and Spirit that has enabled men and women for over 2000 years to live and work together, sharing a common life, a common purpose, an 'ever-rolling stream' of living water, flowing out into the parched lives of others— soothing, cooling, invigorating, transforming, flowing on to the beginning and end of all life, God himself.

What our world needs is not castaways, artificially thrown together, but people drawn by love, shaped by love, empowered by love, to reach out and draw others into the life God intended all to know and enjoy. That truly is 'back to basics'. Whether we are willing to be agents of it is up to us. The choice is ours.

Do nothing from selfish ambition or conceit, but in humility regard others as better than yourselves. Let each of you look not to your own interests, but to the interests of others. Let the same mind be in you that was in Christ Jesus.
Philippians 2:3–5

Lord, I would like to live in a world where everyone loved and cared for one another. Where each person was given dignity, understanding and respect. Where no one lorded it over others, or took advantage of the weak, but respected the feelings and aspirations of each individual, getting alongside them to enable them to fulfil their hopes and dreams. I would like to live in a world where people walked hand in hand, where doors were open, and hearts too. Where the good things of life were seen as gifts to be shared, and not possessions to be hoarded. A world where there were no strangers, no castaways, but all were friends, all part of a community built on love and service, the kingdom of heaven reflected here on earth. I would like to live in a world like that, but the world I live in seems so fragmented, selfish and cruel. 'Survival of the fittest' rules, and there is little room for the weak, the difficult, the despairing. No time to reach out and lift up those who have fallen; instead it is a matter of pushing ahead, getting on, getting through.

And yet, here and there I see signs of new life, signs of the kingdom of heaven in spite of the power struggles of earth—individuals, groups, communities, who have taken to heart and hand the way you set before us when you were here on earth, who have allowed the power of your Spirit to fill them and enable them to share in the ministry of the kingdom. Not an easy option, not a comfortable alternative, but the way that leads to life. I would like to live in that new world, to share in your kingdom, so give me the strength and the courage to be part of it, right here where I am.

Jesus said, 'Whoever serves me must follow me, and where I am, there will my servant be also.'
JOHN 12:26

Chapter 3

'THE END IS NIGH'—OR IS IT?

He is always there at the entrance to the busy London tube station, the old man with his sandwich board carrying dire warning about the end of the world: 'The end is nigh' emblazoned in large black letters. Most people walk straight past him without a look, having far more important things on their mind than the end of the world. Others, especially tourists, look curiously at him, wondering what it is all about. Some raise their eyebrows or shrug their shoulders, while one or two pat him on the shoulder and have a word with him. I find it interesting to observe the various reactions, so I always look out for him and his board. Recently I was coming up from the tube behind a group of young people who were laughing and joking, obviously enjoying their visit to London. When they saw the old man and his board they pointed and began to make fun of him. The old man glared at them and stood his ground: 'You can laugh now, but you won't laugh then!' But his words were wasted. The youngsters had gone on their way, eager to sample the mighty city.

During the early summer of 1999 I met many people who were not laughing about the prospect of the end of the world; in fact they were very anxious. They had not met my old man with his sandwich board, but were taken up with the predictions of a 16th-century physician and astrologer named Michel de Notredame, known as Nostradamus, who had published a sort of *Old Moore's Almanac* predicting the end of the world, and giving descriptions of events that would precede it. His most famous work was his seven-volume *Centuries*—a future history of the world. Some of his predictions did appear to come true, and he was both feared and revered. When he died, as and where he had predicted, even more people took notice, and began to study his work closely.

Nostradamus was a master of the enigmatic, giving all sorts of get-out clauses in his prophecies, yet interest in his predictions has continued to this present day, not least because of the one for the seventh month of 1999: 'The year of 1999, the seventh month, from the sky will come a great King of Terror.' Read into that what you will, but with the advent of the millennium and all the talk of 'gloom and doom', plus media coverage of the writings of Nostradamus, people began to wonder whether, if, perhaps, and what...

Articles appeared in the papers, discussions were held, special television programmes were made, to make sure we were all clued up about the possibility of the end of the world in July. To ease the tension there were cartoons, comedy sound-bites and headlines, but the whole thing caused a great unease, and, among many young people, fear. The weekend before the so-called 'end of the world', one newspaper had on its front page, 'World ends—if not, we will be back next Sunday'. It then went on to say, 'Don't bother to set your alarm clock on Wednesday night, folks. Oh, and you can cancel the milk from Thursday for the world will end on July 1st...'. A very jokey way of putting it, but for vulnerable frightened people, it just added further anxiety.

The predicted day came, and went. A headline the next day read 'End of the world not quite so nigh' and the article that followed said:

> Doomsday came and went yesterday without the apocalyptic results predicted by Nostradamus, the sixteenth-century apothecary and pessimist... In Britain most people were more relaxed. One of the few signs of preparation for the end of the world was a man who sat all day on the Sussex Downs clutching his Bible. London's Survival Shop said there had been a bit of a rush to buy water filters...

Perhaps through all this some people did think seriously about the end of the world, their world; did wonder 'what next?' Yet from my own observations and conversations it seemed that people just brushed it all off, and settled down again into their own mode of life. Perhaps the non-event laid another layer of indifference concerning the end or beginning of anything outside what can be experienced here and now.

In the main, I feel the Christian Church lost out on the opportunity to address the issue of the end time with people who at least showed some interest or concern. Looking back on conversations I had at the time, I have to ask myself whether I did try hard enough to get inside their thinking, to set out the biblical teaching on the end of the world, or to point firmly enough to the need for personal response to Christ here and now. Did it matter to me enough to pursue it? And what does that say about me? I need to reflect on that, not because of what Nostradamus said, but because of what Jesus Christ says, and the challenge and opportunity he offers, which he has charged his followers with sharing.

We do not know the date or time when this world will be wound up, but it will be in God's good time and not ours. What matters is whether we are ready to meet him, and what preparation we are making. Life is very transient, our hold on it is fragile. Whether the end of the world for all of creation comes today or tomorrow, we do not know, but for some people today will be their last, and their world will end. Death is no respecter of persons, old or young, fit or sick, rich or poor. The message of scripture is clear and positive—'Be ready!' The offer of new life through Christ is abundantly made clear. So what are we doing about it while we have time?

Then the sign of the Son of Man will appear in heaven, and then all the tribes of the earth will mourn, and they will see 'the Son of Man coming on the clouds of heaven' with power and great glory. And he will send out his angels with a loud trumpet call, and they will gather his elect from the four winds, from one end of heaven to the other... But about that day and hour no one knows, neither the angels of

heaven, nor the Son, but only the Father… Keep awake therefore, for you do not know on what day your Lord is coming.
MATTHEW 24:30–31, 36, 42

Lord, if I knew just how long I had here on earth I would pace myself better, make sure all my affairs were in order, leave nothing to chance. If I knew when you would be returning I would prepare carefully and joyfully as I do when I go on holiday, making sure my passport is up to date, the tickets paid for, the case dusted down, labelled and packed. If I knew it was to be the end of the world I would warn my friends and neighbours, urge them to put their trust in you, get right with you. Whoever I met, whether I knew them or not, I would tell them about you, I would not want anyone to be lost when there is such a marvellous alternative. If I knew, then it would affect the way I live today, it would give me just the incentive I need to pray, to read, to study, to write, to go, to do, to be, to change from 'one day I will' to 'now I will'. But I don't know, and so I think and act as though it will never happen, nothing will change, there will always be time.

Yet time will run out for me, for the world. You will return—and then? Today I have all the time in the world, all the opportunities, and all the power I need. What am I waiting for, I wonder? Help me to face up to and answer that question now, before it is too late.

Now concerning the times and the seasons, brothers and sisters, you do not need to have anything written to you, for you yourselves know very well that the day of the Lord will come like a thief in the night.
1 THESSALONIANS 5:1–2

Chapter 4

WRITTEN IN
THE BOOK

Life is in full swing, everything as normal for some unsuspecting man
or woman, then suddenly they feel a tap on their shoulder, hear a gasp
of amazement from those around them, and they realize something
very unusual has happened, which seems to concern them. They turn
and see a smiling man carrying a big red book. They are overcome by
a variety of emotions—surprise, delight, excitement, disbelief, even a
touch of fear. Struggling to take in what is happening, they find themselves propelled forward as the smiling man with the big red book says,
'Tonight... this is your life.' As the truth begins to dawn, the picture
fades, and then we see our now well-primed candidate walk-ing on to
a stage, full of confidence, accepting the applause of the audience and
gathered family and friends around them, to hear the contents of that
big red book brought to life—their life, from birth until now.

'This is Your Life' is one of the best-loved television shows. Each
week one of a whole amazing variety of men and women, from every
walk of life, becomes the centrepiece of the programme, and we
discover what has led up to him or her becoming the person they are
today. There are those who have achieved great success and fame
and led distinguished careers. We meet pop stars, actors, musicians,
writers, sportsmen and women. Others have been involved in great acts
of bravery, service, or dedication to others. Some have been shot into
the news spotlight by some special action, and sometimes (I always
find these the most interesting) we meet a so-called 'ordinary' person
who has devoted their life to caring for others, in a quiet unassuming

manner, proving what one person can achieve who gives themselves totally and selflessly. We sit at home, revelling in it all, for nothing pleases us more than finding out what makes our fellow human beings 'tick'. Through the wonder of television we are allowed a front row seat to witness the unfolding of the story, to meet the supporting cast of another's life, and to pass our judgment on it.

But of course we do not get the whole story, only parts, and these the positive and most complimentary, for that is the nature of the programme; and who would agree to appear on it if anything less than worthy should be revealed?

Reading the newspaper day by day I see many accounts of lives revealed, often sordid and sad—such things sell newspapers. It seems that there are always those willing to 'dish the dirt' on people in the public eye or who, for whatever reason, have made the headlines. I find it so sad and unnecessary, but when I raise this I am told it is in the interest of the public to know. Perhaps in some cases it is, but do we need to know every minute detail of another's failings? Would I like it to happen to me or to one of my loved ones? Would you?

All of us are a mixture, whoever we are. There are things in our lives that give us pleasure, that we can be proud of. We have our successes; we build good and lasting relationships, contribute to the community and the life of society. These are the visible credit ratings of our lives. But we all know there is another side as well—our failures, our weaknesses, the regrets, even parts of our personality we may refuse to acknowledge. What if the whole story was told? How would we feel about it? What could we do about it? Quite a frightening prospect! Perhaps there is something in us all which makes us feel that one day we can sort it all out. It will be all right, our credits will outweigh our debits.

But then life is not like that, not according to God anyway, and it is to him that we will give account. We are an open book to God. He knows everything about us, every detail of our lives, every thought, every action, every circumstance. He never views us as a 'This is Your Life' candidate, nor as a paragraph in the daily paper, but entirely as we are. It is a frightening thought, until we realize what he has done for us, that out of love for us he sent Jesus to save us, to rescue us, to give us a new life. We cannot put the book of our life straight, but we can put it into the hands of the one who will and does, if we ask him. 'Old fashioned theology,' some would say. 'Eternal love,' I would reply, love which never goes out of date, but is always valid for those who wish to avail themselves of it.

Sometimes I meet people whose picture of God is of a stern, unforgiving judge, ready to dismiss any who fail to meet the standard he has set before them, turning his face away from them. But God is not like that! He does not say, 'I will love you if or when,' but 'I love you because I love you.' More than this, he knows our heart, he knows our longings, and he understands; he loves us, and he forgives us, and that is the really amazing truth. Too good to be true? No, gloriously true for all who will accept it. The apostle Paul, who for years strove to win God's approval, and got it all wrong, was knocked sideways when he discovered that it was not what he had done or not done that counted, but accepting the love of God through Jesus. He was converted, turned around, and life was never the same again. He was a free man, freed by the forgiving love poured out for him. He could write and explain it to others like this: 'God proves his love for us in that while we were still sinners Christ died for us' (Romans 5:8).

Bishop Richard Holloway in his book *The Way of the Cross* (Fount, 1986) says:

> Jesus is for us. He is on our side. He did not come to condemn us but to save us. He is here for our sake. And this is where the mystery of the cross is at its most powerfully effective. Part of the redemptive strategy of God was to shock us into an awareness of our true condition... And as the scales fall from our eyes... then honesty and contrition begin to sweep through us. Now we know. At last the truth sets us free. (*pp. 98–99*)

We can accept ourselves, because God accepts us. We can enjoy a new life, not because of our frantic efforts to try and balance the books, because that has all been taken care of by God. As Richard Holloway goes on to say:

> Now we can receive the gift. It is, indeed, co-active with our contrition. So Christ in us forgives all that is past and strengthens us to find that amendment of life, that real Christian maturity we seek. As we turn more and more to the Christ within us, his personality permeates ours, his radiance gradually burns through the protective devices we have set up against him and other people, and one day we are free, redeemed, saved by the cross of Christ. (p. 99)

The radiant love of God in Christ demonstrated for us on the cross enables us to stand before God without being afraid. We do not need to hide away, play games, make excuses or try to close our eyes to what we are. He knows all about us; but we are forgiven, we are loved for ever and we can know that freedom, that redeeming love, this very moment.

When God says, 'This is your life, Margaret Cundiff', he does not look at all the good things in it, nor at the bad. He does not need to look at all, because he knows, but he sees my life in the light of his love for me in Jesus. I am as precious as that, now and for all eternity. The same offer applies to every human being, whoever they are; with the one proviso that they accept the gift of love, unreservedly, wholeheartedly, and with thanks. No more he asks, no less he demands.

O Lord, you have searched me and known me.
You know when I sit down and when I rise up;
    you discern my thoughts from far away.
You search out my path and my lying down,
    and are acquainted with all my ways.
PSALM 139:1–3

Father, my life is an open book before you, there is nothing that can be hidden. You have known me from my very beginning, my inclinations, thoughts and actions, they are all recorded. Because you love me you do not leave me to wallow in despair, or become blind to my own failings. You encourage me to walk in your ways, strengthening me that I might overcome temptation. You lift me up, drawing me into your forgiving, healing presence, breathing your Spirit into me, restoring me, enabling me to live as your child, secure in your love. So with grateful thanks I commit all that I am and all that I will be into your safe keeping through Jesus Christ, your son, my Lord and Saviour, for ever and ever. Amen.

Then I said, 'Here I am;
in the scroll of the book it is written of me.
I delight to do your will, O my God;
your law is within my heart.

PSALM 40:7–8

Chapter 5

THE THINKING ANGEL

Bellagio. Just to see or speak that name instantly conjures up a picture of beauty, colour, delight, a feeling of warmth and happiness, a state of utter relaxation. I am instantly transported back to the summer of 1999 to that little town nestling on the shore of Lake Como in Italy, and a charming old-fashioned hotel opposite the ferry point which was the hub of comings and goings from and to all the delightful places around the lake. Music and laughter drifting up from the streets, the smell of Italian food and coffee, and across the blue lake the sight of the elegant Villa Carlotta. And beyond that the mountains, dotted with trees and houses, here and there a church, a winding road, inviting all who would come and sample their charms.

Not all places live up to their name and the expectations they arouse as you turn the pages of the holiday brochures, but Bellagio surpassed all that I had seen or read. It was 'out of this world', and as soon as we had arrived and unpacked I relaxed completely, drawn into its spell. Books remained unread, letters unwritten, the world forgotten as we allowed Bellagio to take us where it would, and always it was good. Even I, avid taker of holiday snaps that I am, often left the camera in the bottom of the bag because what I was seeing with my eyes was too special to attempt to capture it with a camera, I did not want anything to interfere with those magic moments. Everything around had a story to tell, and I knew I had to give my full attention so as not to miss anything; to relax into it all so as to discover what it was all about. I was enchanted, excited by every new discovery, so much so that my daughter Alison who was with me suggested I get a job with the Bellagio Tourist Office, because I was doing such an enthusiastic promotion!

On our last day I was determined to find a souvenir that would remind me of that place, to keep alive the memories, to retain that sense of being part of it all. We strolled round the streets gazing into shop windows, climbing up the narrow side streets, opening doors and dropping down into veritable Aladdin's caves of treasures of all sorts and sizes (prices too). Then we saw them all, in the middle of a window crammed with all sorts—a tray of tiny wooden angels.

'That's what I want, an angel, a guardian angel!'

Alison agreed. 'Yes you do, Mum, you certainly need a guardian angel to keep an eye on you!'

We were in, and the smiling shop assistant was eager to help us. 'I'd like one of the angels, one of those in the window.'

She placed the tray in front of us and said, 'And would you like to see the others?'

Others? She produced from the cupboard beneath the counter more trays, more angels, dozens of them. All the same size, but some plain carved wood, others painted, and yet others in gold. 'They are all different, look.' So they were. Each had its own unique feature or occupation. There were some playing a variety of instruments, smiling, singing, others looking more serious, reading books of various sizes. I was spoilt for choice. Alison and I gazed at all those angels. How could we decide which one it was to be?

Then the shop assistant came to our rescue. She lifted out one of the angels and held it on the palm of her hand. 'This is my favourite, it's called the thinking angel.' A plain wooden angel, finger on lip, with a book held under her arm. I couldn't resist her, and as Alison remarked, 'You could certainly do with one of those!' So the choice was made, the thinking angel it was, and she was well wrapped up to ensure she travelled safely from Bellagio back to north Yorkshire the following morning.

Now she sits on our mantelpiece, thinking—a permanent reminder of a happy summer holiday in Italy. Attached to her back is a small golden cord which could be wings or a heart, depending on the angle you view her from; or maybe it's something as mundane as a means of hanging her up—but I prefer the more romantic idea of wings or hearts. She gives me great food for thought, and seeing her thinking makes me think as well.

Perhaps one of the greatest gifts of that summer holiday in Italy was that everything was geared to slowing down, and reflecting on life, affording the perfect conditions to do so. Everyday life is not so conducive, with far too many distractions, of routine, of demands, of being what I am in the community. On holiday I was just another holidaymaker; time was mine, with no routine, no responsibilities. It was so easy there, but holidays come to an end, the pace of life resumes and quickens. Yet the sight of my thinking angel, who now looks as perfectly at home here in north Yorkshire as she did with her companions in Bellagio, provides a constant challenge to me to make time to think, to reflect.

Angels in scripture always seem so busy, giving messages, issuing commands and warnings, appearing and disappearing, singing, proclaiming and praising. I have not yet found a reference to one whose sole occupation is thinking. But then maybe I have not looked carefully enough, or perhaps not noticed that they are there. What I do know is that thinking angels are to be found right here on earth. They do not rush around loudly, proclaiming their presence, demanding to be heard, but are quiet, unassuming ordinary people—thinkers, listeners, encouragers, people of prayer and godly wisdom, those who are close to the heartbeat of God. They come gently to our aid and calm us, free us from the frenetic busyness which, if allowed to go unchecked, can destroy us. Thank God for thinking angels, God's messengers who by their presence cool and curb our fevered hearts and mind, give us space and time and so enable us to rediscover 'the silence of eternity, interpreted by love'.

I will open rivers on the bare heights,
and fountains in the midst of the valleys;
I will make the wilderness a pool of water,
and the dry land springs of water.

I will put in the wilderness the cedar,
the acacia, the myrtle and the olive;
I will set in the desert the cypress,
the plane and the pine together,
so that all may see and know,
all may consider and understand,
that the hand of the Lord has done this,
the Holy One of Israel has created it.

ISAIAH 41:18–20

Lord, the constant pressures and stresses which we both make and take upon ourselves, and which others thrust upon us, can turn our lives into a wilderness, a desert. To try and find escape we rush madly from one point to another, only to find our way blocked, or the trail false. The hardest thing to do is to stop and think, to look beyond the barren landscape of our own narrow view. Yet it is only as we do that we can see the signs of hope and life you have provided, to sustain, encourage and renew us. We need to know deep within us your life-giving Spirit, bringing fresh springs of understanding, deep-rooted security, the appreciation of beauty, the richness of all creation. In your love and mercy you reach out and bring us to the point of that discovery through your word, through people, through events, the ordinary and the extraordinary—an item, an incident, a sight, a sound. You place your finger on our lips, so that we might stop, think, understand, and know that it is you, our creator, redeemer, sustainer, and our God.

You show me the path of life.
In your presence there is fullness of joy;
in your right hand are pleasures for evermore.

PSALM 16:11

Chapter 6

MAN OF THE PEOPLE— MAN OF GOD

There are those who strive for public acclaim, influence, acceptance, even love. Those who cultivate attitudes, and mannerisms which will endear them to the public, who aspire to the title 'man (or 'woman') of the people'. They are found in every walk of life, but particularly in the realms of public life, of political cut and thrust. Photographs of such people with babies or the elderly, or holding hands with sick or distressed people, are commonplace. The sight of someone in the public eye dressed in the garb of a workman or standing at the 'coal face' of difficult and dangerous activity is aimed to convince us of their sincerity, and concern. We, the general public, are not taken in, are we? We see all this as being at its best a sort of game, at its worst an attempt to gain our confidence by deception. There are also those who would seek to win our minds and souls, by words of eloquence, assuming a 'hot line' to God which is denied to us lesser mortals. They proclaim a state of holiness we could never attain to, but perhaps if we wait around we may receive some crumbs from their table of wisdom and goodness! As the wise adage puts it, however, 'You can fool all the people some of the time, and some of the people all of the time, but you cannot fool all of the people all of the time.' The hypocrite—the play actor—is sooner or later uncovered and discarded.

The true man or woman of the people, the faithful and holy man or woman of God, does not have to strive for recognition, to posture or shout. Such people are recognized, listened to, loved and followed, even by those who would not claim any political or religious allegiance, but who recognize the response of heart to heart, truth, clarity, goodness and hope. In Cardinal Basil Hume we knew such a man. A monk, then abbot, bishop, cardinal, he could have seemed detached from 'the man in the street', living out life in the modern world with all its snares and pitfalls, glitter and grime. And yet we knew he understood, he was one with us, and could draw us into a better relationship with each other, with the world, and with God. That was his gift to us, the gift he had received from God. It was nothing to do with people's faith or lack of it, he touched where they were needing and hurting, he spoke by what he was as well as what he said, and he was clearly understood. When he was told of his terminal cancer he was honest and open about it. He could speak of his own feelings of darkness and fear, and that in itself touched so many who experienced their own darkness and fear. He was also able to bring them with him to a place of trust and confidence, sharing about those times which he described as 'when the curtain came down', but going on to say, 'But I wasn't worried, because I knew what was behind that curtain.'

Early in 1999 he had written in the *Daily Telegraph* about his hopes and fears for the new millennium, the millennium he had hoped to see, and his words were prophetic as we look back on the changeover from 1999 to 2000. He wrote this:

> A firework has a story to tell. It soars up into the sky, brilliant and colourful, an expression of the joy that is ours as we celebrate a special occasion. But its brilliance is shortlived. A charred stick falls to the ground. That is all that is left. I fear that the story of the firework may tell us what it will be like when the celebrations heralding the new Millennium are over. What will be left?

He wrote of the need for spiritual values, and their importance for all of us:

On our pilgrim way through life, we walk, blind and uncertain, often going down byways signposted 'money' or 'power' or 'pleasure', perhaps thinking here we will find all the happiness we desire. Or we might argue that life's pilgrim way actually simply leads to death, the bleakness of the cemetery or crematorium… It is then that we may discover that other pilgrim coming from the opposite direction with an astonishing claim. 'I am the Way, the Truth and the Life,' he said. To see him is, in some manner, to have discovered God himself. That is the pilgrim whose entry into our world 2000 years ago we are preparing to celebrate next year. It is this that gives me and many others the real reason for celebrating and enjoying the fireworks. Forget this reason, or ignore it, and we shall be left only with lots of charred sticks and no more.

At Cardinal Hume's funeral in June 1999 his friend John Crowley, Bishop of Middlesbrough, spoke of him as being a 'deeply loved rock of spiritual strength', and of how the Cardinal had spoken so openly and honestly about the prospect of his dying and death, so releasing others to talk about such subjects. Death lost its taboo, the millennium its urgency, and what really mattered was how to live the good life and die the good death. Bishop John reminded us that the Cardinal had a deep and growing concern that 'the judgment on our age might finally be, we were clever but not wise'. As I, along with so many others, watched the funeral service on television, and listened to those words, I was challenged to look at my own life and lifestyle, and realized how often I try to be clever rather than allow God's wisdom to speak. I give in to the temptation to leave God out of my reckoning and do things my own way. Those words brought me up sharp, and I am grateful that they did.

It seems a long time now since the Cardinal was among us, that time when we were given the chance to listen, to change and be changed. Life goes on, the millennium has come, and so much clamours for our attention, yet his message is still relevant, for it is the message of the one who is 'the way, the truth, and the life', Jesus Christ himself. We can allow the spark that was kindled in our hearts to be nourished, renewed, and fired with new life, or we can choose the noise and brilliance of our own light to bang and flame for a brief time, before we become just charred sticks and no more.

As I think again of all that surrounded those last weeks of the life of Cardinal Hume, as I re-read his words, and those of others who wrote about him, I am encouraged to step out more confidently on my pilgrim way, looking forward to the future, whatever it may bring, secure that God holds the future, holds me, and everyone who will trust him and obey him, for all eternity. Dates and digits change, but God abides, reigns and saves, and gives us reminders, examples and challenges through those who have finished their pilgrim walk, and passed through to the other side of the curtain and into his glorious presence for ever.

Even though I walk through the darkest valley,
I fear no evil;
for you are with me,
your rod and your staff—
they comfort me.
You prepare a table before me
in the presence of my enemies;
you anoint my head with oil;
my cup overflows.
Surely goodness and mercy shall follow me
all the times of my life,
and I shall dwell in the house of the Lord
my whole life long.

PSALM 23:4–6

Lord, as we travel the pilgrim way, sometimes we stumble and fall, we lose heart, are distracted and disheartened. But you provide us with strength and light, you renew us through the living flames of the example of men and women who walk the same road, lighting our path, opening it up, drawing us on. Then they surge ahead. They have fulfilled their calling, and now we must carry that torch of faith and love so that others stumbling along behind us may also find strength and light on their way. Give us power to fulfil our calling, that we may not fail or fall.

Again Jesus spoke to them, saying, 'I am the light of the world. Whoever follows me will never walk in darkness but have the light of life.'
JOHN 8:12

'Let your light shine before others, so that they may see your good works and give glory to your Father in heaven.'
MATTHEW 5:16

Chapter 7

WHY ARE YOU AFRAID?

Lions and tigers are awesome and frightening creatures—powerful, fast, aggressive hunters. Lions and tigers command respect—and distance! They are beautiful creatures, but best viewed from a very safe position, in a safari jeep, or from behind bars. I remember as a child seeing a man enter a cage of lions at a circus. I thought he was very foolish; after all I was familiar with the monologue 'Albert and the Lion', and look what happened to poor Albert. I certainly would have taken no such risks, in spite of being a very adventurous child. From time to time I see news reports of people being eaten by lions or killed by tigers in far-off places, but occasionally nearer home a so-called 'tame' animal has turned and attacked its keeper, causing dreadful injuries and sometimes death. But can you blame the animal? It is its nature to hunt and attack.

When an escaped lion was seen around Barnsley in south Yorkshire stalking the Pennine foothills, naturally people got very worried indeed. In fact there were so many sightings of the ferocious beast that it became known as 'the beast of Birdwell', named after the village where it had been seen. Pets and children were kept indoors, and the area scanned for its whereabouts. Then at last he was cornered, or rather came out to give himself up, very pleased to be the centre of attention. He was no lion but an old ginger dog called Rocky suffering from eczema. Because of his skin complaint his owner had had to have some of his fur shaved, leaving him with a ginger mane and a lion like tassel on the end of his tail. Rocky, the old rottweiler-retriever, plodded along, quite content with his lot and the world in general. He certainly would not have hurt anyone, he was just content to play. Everyone took it in good part. Rocky got his moment of fame, with his picture in the papers and appearing on television, and it made a rather nice story for all to enjoy.

Before you ask how anyone could have imagined an old dog to be a hungry lion, ask yourself what you would have thought in the same circumstances? From a distance the old dog showed all the characteristics of a fearsome lion—the tell-tale signs of mane and tail, the feline gait, it was not until someone got near that Rocky was revealed for what he was—and had been all the time.

In the run-up to the millennium there was an air of foreboding, of something nasty waiting to do us harm, something more threatening than a lion, real or imaginary, worse than any wild beastie or something that goes bump in the night. It was the millennium bug. Not a tangible thing, not a virus, but the threat of what would happen if the computer or electronic systems failed to recognize the year 2000. There were dire warnings of complete shut downs, chaos on land, sea and in the air, the collapse of vital facilities; and the bug grew to alarming proportions in people's minds. Some unscrupulous organizations and people took advantage of others' fear of disaster, playing on their anxieties, and then offering—at an inflated price—to deal with them. Fortunately, reputable organizations and the government worked together and precautions were taken not only to deal with any 'bug' but to inform and educate the public, so we could face up to the possibilities well informed and well armed. The bug was reduced to manageable size, fiction gave way to fact, and in the event our fears were unfounded. Again it was a matter of seeing things as they really were, and not viewed through fear-tinted glasses.

Fear distorts the truth and holds us captive, if we let it. Those worries deep inside us, the problems that seem so huge, so menacing, the chilling anxieties that sap our energy and confidence, holding us in their power—and they always seem worse in the middle of the night—assume giant proportions. Yet as we do face up to them, and look them in the eye, we often find they are not what they seemed. They are minor and manageable, we can beat them. What also helps (certainly it does for me) is to share those fears and anxieties with a good friend, being prepared to listen and take action, and not to keep going over the old ground again and again. Two are better than one in dealing with fear and anxiety, especially when you have confidence in that other one beside you. Together you can advance on the problem, and meet it head on, rather than keep running away from the situation or allowing it to defeat you.

Jesus' disciples were often afraid, even when he was there beside them. At times they allowed their fears to blot out the sense of his presence, and the memory of their past experience of his power. How could they be so stupid when he was always with them, always available? How could they forget his promises, his faithfulness, his love? Because they were human, just as we are. We too may be followers of Jesus Christ, committed to him, knowing his love and power, but sometimes, like those disciples, when the chips are down, or seem to be, confidence and trust go out of the window. Over and over again Jesus reminded them of his presence with them, even when they did not realize it: 'Take heart, it is I, do not be afraid'; 'Why are you afraid, have you no faith?' 'Do not let your hearts be troubled, and do not let them be afraid.' When they hid behind locked doors he broke through their fear with 'Peace be with you', and 'Remember, I am with you always, to the end of the age'—his promise when he commissioned them to go and share the good news. These are words we do well to take to ourselves, reminding ourselves of those promises and assurances. Then we can face whatever confronts us, real or imagined, knowing that through him we will overcome, we will know the victory.

When it was evening on that day, the first day of the week, and the doors of the house where the disciples had met were locked for fear of the Jews, Jesus came and stood among them and said, 'Peace be with you.' After he said this, he showed them his hands and his side.

Then the disciples rejoiced when they saw the Lord. Jesus said to them again, 'Peace be with you. As the Father has sent me, so I send you.'

JOHN 20:19–21

Lord, sometimes when I look out at the world I feel afraid, I don't know which way to turn. I am alone and lost, or so it seems. I want to run away, but where, how? Those things, situations, people, feelings—out there—are menacing, threatening to hurt me, even destroy me. I feel as if shadows are creeping up on me, and I dare not face them. There is no escape.

Then I remember the promises you made when you were here on earth to people just like me, the promises you kept and still keep. You stilled the storms, calmed the passions, brought order out of chaos, gave peace and assurance, won the victory over sin and death. You stand here beside me and ask, 'Why are you afraid?' and I know there is no need to fear. I can face all that lies ahead because you are with me. You have been there, you have dealt with it already. Slowly the fears subside. Now the shadows disappear, the horizon I see is no longer dark but light, and I can go forward, knowing that you will go with me, my guide, my strength, my peace and my joy for ever.

Jesus said, 'I have said this to you, so that in me you may have peace. In the world you face persecution. But take courage: I have conquered the world.'

JOHN 16:33

Chapter 8

NOT TOO BIG
TO SAY SORRY

It was not the best of days, not the sort of day you would choose to go
out, but the invitation was too good to miss. One of the local
supermarkets' 'special offers' leaflet had come through the letter box,
and picking it up off the mat I noticed a product listed which I use
regularly, at almost half price. So in spite of the weather, in spite of my
list of things I needed to do, I headed into the supermarket for my
special offer—to be met with empty spaces where that particular
product was usually to be found. Never mind, I could always call in
tomorrow, which I duly did, with the same result. I sought out the
manager, who smiled at me rather wearily. He had met many customers
like me that morning, and explained that the special offer had sold out
quickly yesterday, and today, but as for tomorrow—well there would be
a large delivery.

Early next day I made my way, full of optimism, to the store, only to
meet the same empty shelves, and the promise, 'Come back about
eleven, there will be plenty then.' I did, but there wasn't, and so, not
in the best of tempers, I drove back home and put pen to paper,
directing my complaint to the sales director at the head office, for obviously something was wrong in their administration and distribution
departments.

I expected to receive a standard 'we have noted your comments and
regret any inconvenience which may have been caused' letter, rather
like one of those so-called 'apologies' for late-running trains and
planes, but the letter which came a few days later was both personal

and detailed. It was obvious they had spent time and trouble investigating my complaint, had not covered up or made excuses, but admitted they were having problems and outlined the action they were taking, plus enclosing a compensation voucher because of their failure to fulfil the advertising offer. I was impressed, and not only by the voucher, but by the way they had dealt with one customer's complaint. I felt that I had been listened to, that my comments had been acted upon. They had not tried to brush off or dismiss my complaint, but had dealt with it, and were big enough to say sorry. A feeling of warm satisfaction came over me, even a touch of smugness that I had been right to pursue matters, to give them the opportunity of showing just how important it was to admit when they were at fault. After all, 'the customer is always right'—in my case 100 per cent right.

But these things have a way of rebounding, and this was no exception. Suddenly it was as though the ball was hit back into my court, issuing me with the challenge, 'Yes, that's fine, but how well do you deal with complaints, when you are faced with your mistakes and shortcomings? What about those times you fail to live up to the claims you make, the expectations you engender?' Taken off guard I could only concede defeat. There had been no time to offer a defence, for I knew well enough the times I try to cover up, turn a deaf ear, blame someone else, and refuse to acknowledge the possibility that I may be at fault. The problem will evaporate, or so I hope, or be overtaken by something else providing a welcome diversion, so that I can neatly sidestep the problem. Yet I know in my heart of hearts it does not work like that. If something is unresolved, then relationships are marred, even broken. Others are hurt and disappointed, and worse still, the Lord I profess to love and serve is discredited. In effect, I put a stumbling block in the path of his love and mercy to prevent them reaching through.

Excuses are as old as Adam, and the results writ large through the pages of history, and in the history we are making this very day for those who come after us. The excuses given by Adam and Eve to God may seem to us ridiculous in our day and age. When asked by God whether he had eaten of the tree, Adam replied, 'The woman whom you gave to be with me, she gave me fruit from the tree and I ate.' In other words, it was God's fault for giving him a partner; and she in turn blamed the serpent: 'The serpent tricked me and I ate' (Genesis 3:12–13). No mention of the fact that she had listened to the creature rather than obeying the creator; and yet we sophisticated men and women of the third millennium still rattle out the same vain excuses, blaming God, each other, and our environment, for our failures and for the consequences that inevitably follow.

Former American President Harry S. Truman kept a sign on his desk which read, 'The buck stops here', as a constant reminder of his accountability, of his willingness to face up to his shortcomings and to deal with them honestly. I remember, as a young and inexperienced personnel officer, being told by my manager—a wise and perceptive lady, 'You are new to this work and all its demands. You will make mistakes, that is for certain, for if you do not make mistakes you will not make anything, but when you do make mistakes, don't try to cover them up or hide them, come to me and I will help you. If you don't tell me, I will not be able to help you, and you will only make the situation worse.' How glad I was of her words and her offer. Many times I would go to her and admit, 'I'm sorry, but…' and she would kindly but firmly sit me down and say, 'Now, tell me, what exactly happened…' and at the end of my account she would sit deep in thought for a few moments and then say briskly, 'The answer to this is…'. I did learn, and as I progressed up the promotion ladder I gave that same advice and help to those who joined our team. And after all these years her words still ring in my ears and heart. I have proved over and over again the truth of them, of the need to be big enough to admit mistakes, to say and be sorry, and begin again in an atmosphere of understanding, trust and support.

My wise friend of long ago is no longer with us, but what she taught and showed me remains. We all need wise friends who will counsel and listen to us, correct and encourage, be there for us—a 'soul friend', spiritual director, or mentor. The title does not matter, but what it means is someone with whom we can be absolutely honest and open, whose guidance we trust, act upon and learn from. And of course we always have access to the wisest friend of all, any time, anywhere, for, as the old hymn puts it, 'What a friend we have in Jesus'. What a friend indeed.

Jesus said, 'Come to me, all you that are weary and are carrying heavy burdens, and I will give you rest. Take my yoke upon you, and learn from me, for I am gentle and humble in heart, and you will find rest for your souls. For my yoke is easy, and my burden is light.'
MATTHEW 11:28–30

Lord, I don't like making mistakes and, even more, I don't like being found out. I like to think I am in control, that I can sort everything out so well, that I know what I am doing. And so it comes as a blow to my pride when I discover that I am at fault, when I make a mess of something, cause problems for others. It is so easy to make excuses, even to put the blame on someone else, when what I need to do is admit I am in the wrong, apologize, and try to gather up the pieces.

But saying 'sorry' is hard. I feel such a fool—what is the expression?— 'eating humble pie'. Not very tasty, not the sort of fare I prefer. It weighs down upon me, so I look for a way of escape, a means of saving my face, salvaging my pride and self-esteem. Where can I go? Who will understand? What can I say?

You know me, and everything about me; you know what I do, how I feel. There are no secrets hidden from you, and yet you invite me to come to you, bringing my burden of failure, guilt and pride, to learn from you, to be released to admit my faults to you and to those I have failed. To know restoration, renewal and strength for the days that lie ahead.

Listen to advice, and accept instruction, that you may gain wisdom for the future.
PROVERBS 19:20

Chapter 9

WHOSE CHILD
IS IT?

Surrounded by a group of bright-eyed, attentive children, I was thoroughly enjoying telling them the story of how Jesus took a child and put it in the place of honour beside him. 'And that is how important you are to him,' I concluded.

A girl put her hand up. 'Mrs Cundiff, was it a boy or a girl?'

I couldn't think for a moment what she was asking, and looked at her rather puzzled. 'Was it a boy or a girl Jesus chose?' she repeated.

Oh dear, I had not reckoned with that one. How many times had I told that story in assemblies over the years, and no one had ever asked me that before. I was stumped. 'It doesn't say.' I answered lamely, while trying to look very positive, but I could see that I had lost their attention. After all, 'a child' meant nothing. They wanted to know what sort of a child, how old, what sort of clothes, what it was doing there, all the sort of personal details that really mattered. Unless they knew, then they could not visualize the scene, the conversation. It was all too abstract, so their minds were now elsewhere, on more important matters.

When I got back home I looked up all the references, but nowhere did it say what sex the child was, or anything about the child, it was... a child. The question had set me wondering. Maybe it had been lost in translation, or to the writers of the Gospel accounts it had not seemed important enough to record. Perhaps the listeners had been so attentive to what Jesus was saying that they had not given 'the child' a second glance; but whatever, the value and importance Jesus placed on children came as a surprise to those around. After all, what use were children? In fact, his disciples shooed them away when they were brought to Jesus for him to touch them; but he reprimanded the disciples for their action and welcomed the children, picking them up, holding and blessing them. He had strong words to say about anyone who would hurt a child, put obstacles in its way or cause it to sin, thereby destroying its innocence, depriving the child of its birthright.

Our courts today rightly demand the highest penalties to be placed upon those who are found guilty of crimes against children, but Jesus issued his solemn warning of a judgment far greater than any court of the land—the condemnation of God, of utter destruction. Children were and are precious gifts, with all the potential needed for a lifetime, and adults have the privilege and responsibility of enabling that potential to be released positively, enabling the child to flourish and develop a happy, well-balanced and mature personality.

In a society where children were often seen as expendable, a burden, only of any value when they could work and contribute to the family income, Jesus gave them a place of honour. They were to be respected and protected. Two thousand years later, as again we read his words, see his concern and hear his dire warnings to those who would offend against children, have we as today's society learned anything? We look aghast at countries where very young children work long hours in factories or on the land, are used as 'sex slaves', are abandoned, neglected, forced into frontline fighting, perverted, denied even basic care, disposed of, regarded as dispensable objects.

We read the horrifying reports, and turn away, saying, 'It would never happen here.' But oh yes, it can, and does, and when the news breaks we can hardly believe it—after all, 'We love children.' We all need to be on our guard to make sure it cannot and does not happen, to be vigilant and aware of the dangers that lurk even in our own neighbourhood. Time after time when the news breaks of some dreadful case concerning children, people say, 'I never thought anything like that could happen here, it's such a nice area, they seemed quiet, decent people…'. Child abuse and neglect, paedophile gangs, drug-related crimes against children, and one of the very frightening trends,

Internet porn offences worldwide—these are all things that we need to use our influence and powers to break.

Trying to trace victims and help them is not always pursued as it might be. One recent report even said, 'It is not an economic use of police resources... identifying the children could prove hugely expensive.' It is easy to condemn the inefficiencies of a system, the mistakes made by what should be caring agencies, the perverted and sick individuals who prey on children. It is easy to hold up our hands in horror and revulsion; but children are the responsibility of all of us. We are all called to love, protect and honour them—not just our own children, or those of families and friends, or those within our church organizations, but all, and especially any we see in need of help. And when we fail to respond wholeheartedly and immediately, we are guilty of neglect, and fall under the condemnation and judgment of God.

I gain so much through my contact with children. They enhance my life, they teach me so much, they are indeed a gift, a blessing. Through them I have a wonderful insight not only into the life of children, but that of adults, seen through the eyes of children. We are all children at heart, and children enable us to remain so. We need their incisive and penetrating observations, with their ability to go to the heart of the matter, their sheer joy and enthusiasm for living. I owe children a great debt every day of my life; and by being actively concerned for those who do not have the opportunities that they should have, whose situations are dire, who are vulnerable without hope or help, I can do something to address the situation, however small and ineffective my contribution may seem. That 'child in the midst' chosen by Jesus stands for every child of every age, and the words Jesus spoke then he speaks right now to you and to me, and demands that we respond as he responds, reminding us too of the penalty of our neglect: that we will be called to account for our failure.

Recently I was with some friends I had known since childhood. We were talking about 'the old days', as people tend to do when they get to our age, recalling some of those who had helped us, guided us, got us out of scrapes, protected us and put us on the right path. At the time we had not appreciated the time and effort they gave, the love and concern they lavished upon us, the very real dangers they had protected us from. One friend said, 'When I think back, and I realize how different things might have been, it's quite frightening. We were so fortunate, weren't we?' Yes we were. There were dangers of many kinds, which as children we were quite oblivious of, but thankfully there were people around who cared and watched and acted, who knew and valued us as individuals, precious, special to them and to God. They enabled us to grow up into adults, and to make our own contribution to life.

The generations come and go, children are born, grow up, become adults, pass on what they have received, of good or ill, the cycle continues. And Jesus says to us, 'You want to know who is the greatest in the kingdom of heaven? This little one standing here beside me— make sure you take good care!'

At that time the disciples came to Jesus and asked, 'Who is the greatest in the kingdom of heaven?' He called a child, whom he put among them, and said, 'Truly I tell you, unless you change and become like children, you will never enter the kingdom of heaven. Whoever becomes humble like this child is the greatest in the kingdom of heaven. Whoever welcomes one such child in my name, welcomes me. If any of you put a stumbling-block before one of these little ones who believe in me, it would be better for you if a great millstone were fastened around your neck and you were drowned in the depths of the sea.'
MATTHEW 18:1–6

Lord, those were fierce words of warning you issued, of judgment and wrath towards those who would hinder or hurt a child. You meant them then, and you mean them now, and they are addressed to me. So I have to ask myself, 'Do I ever put a stumbling block in the way of a child by what I say or do, in the way I respond or fail to respond?' Help me to see all the children I meet through your eyes of love, acceptance, and welcome, to be willing to learn from them and with them. Don't allow me to become indifferent to the reports of suffering children because the terrible problems seem beyond my comprehension or ability to make a difference. Don't allow me to ignore the appeals from those who are seeking to help those in need; but help me instead to see them as opportunities to co-operate in the task of bringing healing, hope and new life, sharing wholeheartedly in every way I can, for your love's sake, and in your name.

And he took them up in his arms, laid his hands on them, and blessed them.
MARK 10:16

Chapter 10

CITY OF GOD

Every capital city in the world has its own unique identity, its own ethos and drawing power, historical, political, material, intellectual, technological. At the centre are thrones and governments, the seats of power, whether from long lines of royal succession, elected first ministers or dictators. We find the financial centre, touching upon the lives of every individual; the business sector, the head offices of companies, and organizations, where decisions taken in the morning can affect the whole world by afternoon. There are cities that by night become playgrounds, drawing those seeking relaxation and pleasure in the theatre, music, the arts. The bright lights of a city seem rich, powerful and pleasurable, but in the shadows lurk evils and hurts, poverty, tragedy, crime, fear and oppression, those who prey upon the weak and defenceless, those who are abused and betrayed. And there is a constant flow of people—those who live and work in the city, and those who are drawn to it, seeking to discover the city, be part of it, accepted by it. London, New York, Tokyo, Paris, Rome, Madrid, Hong Kong, and all the other great teeming centres —I have visited many over the years, and marvelled at city life, tried to discover what was at the heart of them.

When I was given the opportunity to visit Jerusalem, the Holy City, I jumped at the chance. It had been a dream of mine to walk the streets, breathe the air, feel the atmosphere of that spiritual capital where the three great religious faiths converge, Judaism, Islam and Christianity. I will never forget my first sight of Jerusalem. We arrived at night, but were taken to a high vantage point overlooking the city. We could see the dark outlines of buildings, the glittering lights, and hear the sound of the city coming up to meet us, a mixture of traffic, voices and activity. The following morning we woke to bright sunshine, and walked through those narrow streets, visiting sacred places, walking through the noisy market area, full of sounds and smells, people and their wares; and always being aware of suspicious eyes following us, of young soldiers on the alert, covering us, and the atmosphere electric, ready to explode at any moment.

Jerusalem, the Holy City of God, built for his glory, ought to have been a spiritual home for all people, reflecting the holiness and joy of the new Jerusalem, heaven itself; but instead it has become a focal point of bitterness, hatred and, so often, death. We hear of peace moves 'shot in the heart' through the response of violence to violence, the cries of pain and grief mingled with those of hatred and for vengeance. The hopes and longings of God's people, of all nations, throughout the centuries, have been drowned out by conflict. 'Time is a great healer,' it is said, but there are no signs of healing here as the centuries roll by.

Yet for all this, I found in Jerusalem pockets of hope, hidden corners of faith and love, and people who not only prayed for the peace of Jerusalem, but were actively working for it. Hope still hung by a slender, yet unbroken, thread. Looking out at the city our Lord loved so much and lamented over, I could hear again his words of compassion and anguish: 'Jerusalem, Jerusalem, the city that kills the prophets and stones those who are sent to it! How often have I desired to gather your children together as a hen gathers her brood under her wings, and you were not willing' (Matthew 23:37). I could feel that love being poured out for his people, his offer still being extended, in spite of the past history and the present conflicts.

The picture of a mother hen gathering her chicks into the safety and warmth of her own body and drawing them together as a family is a very poignant one. As Jesus expressed his longings, only days before his death, his listeners failed to realize what he was talking about, and what he was offering them. They preferred to boast of the stone structure of the city they were so proud to inhabit, putting their faith in what we would call today 'bricks and mortar', rather than in God's love and forgiveness, the shelter of his wings of mercy. In just a few years, in AD70, Jerusalem would be laid waste, destroyed by the

Romans, the security it had been so proud of reduced to rubble. Not for the first time, nor for the last.

Yet the city of Jerusalem has been restored, raised over and over again, and it still has that magnetic attraction that draws people from every part of the world to it—as it had me. As I stood in the city, with those words of Jesus running through my mind, I prayed for the peace of Jerusalem—the physical peace that all longed for, yet would not release to each other; the peace that was only possible through all men and women recognizing their common citizenship, being willing to live in peace and harmony together. I wondered how long it would be, if ever. How long could this city stand before it was torn apart yet again? It was a dismal and depressing thought. What hope was there for peace?

Then words of Jesus that he spoke in this very city came to me, words of assurance: 'I, when I am lifted up from the earth, will draw all people to myself' (John 12:32). Those prophetic words are being fulfilled every moment of every day, as men and women turn to him, drawn by the power of his love. That love was shown supremely as he was hoisted high on the cross at Calvary, above his beloved city, drawing all people into the company of the citizens of New Jerusalem, the eternal city that the psalmist rejoiced to extol:

> On the holy mount stands the city he founded;
>   the Lord loves the gates of Zion
> more than all the dwellings of Jacob.
> Glorious things are spoken of you,
>   O city of God!'
>   (Psalm 87:1–3)

These words became a personal reality for John Newton, an 18th-century slave trader who came to know that citizenship through the love and power of Jesus, and who could write:

> Saviour, since of Zion's city
> I through grace a member am,
> Let the world deride or pity,

I will glory in thy name.
Fading is the world's best pleasure,
All its boasted pomp and show;
Solid joys and lasting treasure
None but Zion's children know.

The earthly Jerusalem still holds within it the symbols of the divine mystery of love, which will not be discovered by excavating its foundations, examining its treasures or defending its walls, but by looking to the one who by his death upon the cross, and his rising again, gifts us with his peace for now and for all eternity.

I was glad when they said to me,
'Let us go to the house of the Lord!
Our feet are standing
within your gates, O Jerusalem.'
Jerusalem—built as a city
that is bound firmly together.
To it the tribes go up,
the tribes of the Lord,
as it was decreed for Israel,
to give thanks to the name of the Lord.
For there the thrones for judgment were set up,
the thrones of the house of David.
Pray for the peace of Jerusalem:
'May they prosper who love you.
Peace be within your walls,
and security within your towers.'
For the sake of my relatives and friends
I will say, 'Peace be within you.'
For the sake of the house of the Lord our God,
I will seek your good.
PSALM 122

Lord God, it is an awesome thing to stand within the gates of Jerusalem, to walk through the narrow streets of the city and be part of a teeming throng from every part of the world, of all languages and customs, religions and ideologies. With our stout shoes for walking, hats to protect our heads from the sun; carrying our guide books, cameras and bottled water; making sure to keep together, watching our purses; we all the time try to catch a glimpse of you, to hear your voice, for this is your city. There are so many buildings erected to house you, to honour you, all claiming you for their own. But where are you? Where should I look? Where do I begin? You are here now, beside me, within me, wherever I go. You are with me, drawing me to yourself, leading me onward until I come to the New Jerusalem, to dwell with you, for ever.

I saw the holy city, the new Jerusalem, coming down out of heaven from God, prepared as a bride adorned for her husband. And I heard a loud voice from the throne saying, 'See, the home of God is among mortals. He will dwell with them, they will be his peoples, and God himself will be with them.'

REVELATION 21:2–3

Chapter 11

BUT WHAT IF...?

Mary and Joseph sat gazing at the baby Jesus, who was wrapped up and in his wooden cradle. Behind them stood the angel Gabriel, wings outstretched over them all, in a protecting pose. A lovely tableau, the centre-piece of our village carol service—and a historic occasion, for it was to be the last nativity play of the 20th century performed in the village. The part of Mary was taken by six-year-old Rachel, very conscious of her leading role, with four-year-old Matthew playing the part of Joseph. Normally an all-action boy, not known for his ability to sit still for very long, he had been persuaded to be very good and very quiet, and seemed to have got the message. He was a little young for such a major role, but he was the only boy we had, so greatness had been thrust upon him for that evening. Mary, aged ten, who was Matthew's older sister, took the role of Gabriel. She had a number of performances under her belt, knew the story perfectly and how it should be performed, and enjoyed her dramatic role. So the scene was set, to the oohs and aahs of the congregation.

As time went on, the novelty wore off for Matthew, and he began to rock the cradle with his foot; and finding it increasing in speed, pushed it ever harder. Rachel was not amused, and poked him to try to make him stop being so rough with the cradle; but Matthew had got into his swing, literally, and was enjoying himself, regardless of the now more frequent nudges. At last Mary could stand it no longer and came to the defence of her brother by telling Rachel very firmly to stop poking Matthew, at which Rachel told Mary in no uncertain terms that as she was taking the part of Mary, and Matthew was supposed to be Joseph, then if she wanted to stop him upsetting baby Jesus she would. Then followed a heated argument about who should hold the carol sheets. Mary, unable to stand it any more, stalked off into the congregation, but was persuaded to return and resume her position as Gabriel, at which Rachel looked up at her and said very firmly, 'You're not the boss round here!'

I took advantage of the next carol to tell the trio quietly that they were doing very well indeed, and if they could manage to stay in their positions for just a little while longer it would be lovely. Like true little troupers they did, and all was forgiven. They posed for photographs before wriggling out of their costumes and dashing off for their drinks and biscuits. As I said to my husband Peter on the way home, 'I always enjoy nativity plays. It's the same story, but every one has a different twist.' Over the years I have taken part in, arranged, and watched more than I can remember, but what I do remember are the wonderful spontaneous diversions from the script, the pathos and humour, and not least the thought that always comes to mind: 'But what if…?' What if Joseph had at the last moment backed out of his supporting role? What if the shepherds, so engrossed in their 'mini rugby' game, had not listened to the message of the angels, and not made the journey to Bethlehem? What if one of the wise men had chosen to unwrap his gift and decided to take it back home with him? Or if Mary and Joseph had been so anxious to escape into Egypt they had forgotten to take the baby with them? What then?

All these, and many other situations too, have arisen over the years in our retelling of the story—but what if it had really happened like that? What if Mary had rejected God's message? What if Herod had caught up with the family at Bethlehem? What if Simeon had not been in the temple when Mary and Joseph brought Jesus in, and what if Anna had not come at that moment? As we read of the coming of Jesus into the world, hear the familiar words and see it played out, we can take it all for granted, lose the sense of wonder and awe, even let it float over our heads and hearts. Sometimes it takes the words or actions of a child, a slip from the script, a thought that surfaces, to bring us back into focus, to marvel, to praise, and to realize what God has done for us; not just two thousand years ago, but for us here and now, today.

We can argue about dates and times, whether the millennium began on 1 January 2000 or 2001, or even a few years before or after; but it really does not matter, not in the light of God's love and of eternity. God came to live here with us as an ordinary, vulnerable human being, subject to fads and fashions, to temptation, danger and death, yet rising above and beyond it all and drawing us with him through life and death to new life. No one else has ever done that, or ever will, but Jesus, who is 'the same yesterday, today, and for ever'.

For a child has been born for us,
a son given to us;
authority rests upon his shoulders;
and he is named
Wonderful Counsellor, Mighty God,
Everlasting Father, Prince of Peace.
His authority shall grow continually,
and there shall be endless peace
for the throne of David and his kingdom.
He will establish and uphold it
with justice and with righteousness
from this time onwards and for evermore.
The zeal of the Lord of hosts will do this.

ISAIAH 9:6–7

Father, so many 'what ifs' come into my mind as I read again of the coming of your Son Jesus Christ into the world. What if he had come in splendour as King, with unassailable might, leaving no doubt as to your purpose and plan? He could have silenced any opposition with a thunderbolt, destroyed any who stood in his path, ensured his complete safety at all times, under-written his mission with the treasury of heaven, assuring his prominence in the royal courts of the world. It could have all happened in a moment, and I would have bowed low in fear and awe, submitting myself to his rule. What if it had been like that? No need then for his pain and suffering. There would have been no restrictions, no risk, no doubt, no struggle, no death and no choice.

But it was by a very different route that he came. He entered into this world as a baby, carried in the womb of a humble peasant girl for nine months, delivered in an outhouse, facing an uncertain future, amid political, religious and social upheaval, cut off in his prime at 33, dying the death of a common criminal—and for what? To win the love of ordinary, weak, sinful human beings like me; showing, living, giving love, risking everything, even life itself, so that I might know love, life and freedom in this world and the next. May my response to his love always be 'yes', and never 'what if?'

For God so loved the world that he gave his only Son, so that everyone who believes in him may not perish but may have everlasting life.
JOHN 3:16

Chapter 12

AN OUTWARD
AND VISIBLE SIGN

Christmas Eve. The church is ablaze with colour and light. The tall candles are lit on the table, and from every crevice and ledge other tiny candles flicker and dance, like children bobbing with excitement, while the huge Christmas tree in the sanctuary shines on and above the people gathered for the midnight celebration of holy communion. The old familiar carols ring out, voices raised in praise and thanksgiving that 'Christ is born in Bethlehem', and in the prayer that he might be born in us afresh this night.

The preacher, a young man, sits to deliver the sermon. He sits because he is in a wheelchair, the result of the disabling illness which has gradually taken the use of his legs, so that now he can only stand with great effort. Yet this is no tragic story, but one of a battle won against the odds. That young man, Sean, has successfully completed his training as a Church Army officer, and now looks forward to his commissioning and then to taking up his new sphere of work, along with his wife Joy and their two children. When the time comes for the administration of holy communion, my colleague David and I help him into the sanctuary so he can administer a chalice, for we are a team, and never more so than in this Christmas Eve sharing in the deepest way possible through bread and wine.

Christmas morning, and the church is full. We run out of books. We wonder whether there will be enough balloons to go round at the end of the service for all the children to have one. The balloons are fastened to the pulpit, which by now looks like a rainbow-coloured spaceship.

Again the candles blaze, the songs ring out, and the voices of excited children provide a delightful accompaniment. Presents are shown and shared, and each child receives a square of chocolate from this morning's preacher who sits on the steps, surrounded and 'helped' by the children in a practical demonstration of the message of giving and sharing.

Between David and myself sits our greatly loved Reader, Ken, in his cassock, surplice and blue scarf. His smile beams brighter than all the candles put together, and it is reflected by everyone gathered there. It is Christmas morning, and Ken is with us, sharing in the administration of holy communion. All of us are conscious that we are witnessing a miracle, and there are tears of joy and thanksgiving that we are here to witness and share in it. For earlier this year Ken had been diagnosed as suffering from a brain tumour. He underwent surgery, which was only partially successful, and the resultant treatment left him a shadow of his former self. Ken, who had brought such light and love into our midst in the few short years that he and his wife Jean had been with us; Ken, who had given us so much, who had taken us all to his heart, who had been a means of such blessing and encouragement, was being snatched from us so cruelly. He was at his lowest during Holy Week and Easter, a time of grief and sadness for his family, and for the church family. David had written these words on his Easter card to me: 'It feels like Good Friday all the way this year, I know. So much sadness and loss, with Ken's illness, but the Son will shine in our hearts, Easter will appear from behind the cloud…'. The days, weeks and months passed. Physically, Ken grew weaker, unable to continue as Reader, but he was radiant as he shared in worship at most services from his pew, surrounded by loving support. He ministered week by week, blessing us by his faith, his trust, his joy in the Lord. In the summer he and Jean celebrated their golden wedding, and were able then to enjoy a holiday with their family, and through the time God gave were able to do what seemed impossible.

Ken was determined to share in the Christmas celebrations, and the week before he grinned at me and whispered, 'I'm still here!' We all knew that the greatest joy we could share would be to have Ken at

61

Christmas ministering 'up front'—but would it be possible? David worked out all the practical details, where we could put his chair, how he could share in the adminstration; and it ran perfectly. Ken radiated the joy of the Lord, and as each one came up for communion he greeted them, offering them the bread of life, each one individually. Old and young alike came to him, aglow with love and thanksgiving for Christmas, for God's gift of love in Jesus, and for God's gift of love through his servant Ken. At the end of the service he was able to walk down the aisle with us, amid the applause, the singing and the balloons. It was like Easter and Christmas all of a piece. The Son had shone on and in our hearts, the light had come, and God had given us a bonus of blessings.

Reflecting on our Christmas celebrations I was transported back in time to one of the confirmation classes I had attended as a teenager. We were sitting in our vicar's study and he was taking us through the catechism, explaining what a sacrament is, and particularly the sacrament of holy communion which we would soon be sharing in. I have never forgotten those words from the catechism, describing the meaning of the word 'sacrament'—'an outward and visible sign of an inward and spiritual grace given unto us, ordained by Christ himself, as a means whereby we receive the same and a pledge to assure us thereof'. We don't use language like that these days. Confirmation classes follow a very different pattern. And yet when I learned those words I stored them up in my heart, and have pondered on them many times, trying to discover the heart of their meaning. And it was at Christmas 1999, just one week before the new millennium, that they exploded like the stars of heaven in a revelation beyond human explanation. Weakness and suffering were a means of God's grace, shown in bread and wine shared, given and received. Divine love, human love, and amazing, amazing grace came together.

Then he (Jesus) took a cup, and after giving thanks he said, 'Take this and divide it among yourselves, for I tell you that from now on I will

not drink of the fruit of the vine until the kingdom of God comes.'
Then he took a loaf of bread and when he had given thanks, he broke
it, and gave it to them saying, 'This is my body, which is given for
you. Do this in remembrance of me.'
LUKE 22:17–19

*Lord, you shared the everyday things of life and made them holy by your
presence. You gave yourself so that we might enjoy the bread of life, the new
wine of eternity. You put into our hands and hearts the gift of yourself, and
entrust us with sharing you with others, using those same symbols of bread
and wine. Taking, receiving, eating, drinking, giving, celebrating, with you
and one another. As we reach out in faith and love, transform us, make us
holy, make us whole, make us one in your life, in your death and in your risen
power.*

As often as you eat this bread and drink the cup, you proclaim the
Lord's death until he comes.
1 CORINTHIANS 11:26

Chapter 13

COME FLY
WITH ME

My birthday was hovering on the near horizon, the annual addition to the tally of years, causing for my nearest and dearest the problem of how to reward me for such a noteworthy achievement. Most surprises had been tried over the years, with varying success, but nowadays, or nowayears, the ball was put into my court and batted to and fro until some sort of a solution was found—and, I may say, always enjoyed and appreciated. So the inevitable question was tossed casually my way. 'What would you like for your birthday?' I could see from Peter's glazed expression that he was already running through the usual list of smellies, something from the underwear department of a well-known chain store, a CD or tape, maybe a book or magazine subscription, the usual sort of thing. So when I said, 'A kite', it rather threw him.

I saw him do a double take and then he repeated what I had said, slowly with a suspicious note. 'A kite?'

'Yes, a kite.'

'A kite? What do you want a kite for?' A silly question I thought, surely everyone knows what you do with a kite.

'I want a kite to fly it, that's what you do with kites.'

He seemed to get the general idea. 'But why do you want one?'

Patiently I explained that I had wanted a kite for a long time, it was one of those things that had been on my 'one day I will' list, but now the time was right. Well, at least I had decided it was.

Peter gave in. 'And where do you get kites from?' This I had worked out. I knew exactly the place. In fact, I knew the range of kites stocked, because I had spent some time studying them, and would quite happily have any of them—as a starter of course, but that detail could be kept for later.

End of conversation, and I did half wonder whether he had taken me seriously. But then, after all these years of knowing me, I felt he knew when I really meant what I said, however strange it might seem. And on my birthday sure enough, there it was, my kite.

A few days later, with the wind blowing at just the right speed, the kite got its first outing. It took to the air as to the manner born (or manufactured), a joy to behold and hold and direct and marvel at; and if curious passers-by thought it rather strange to see this 'mature woman' having fun and games with a blue and orange kite it did not deter her in the least.

Kite flying is considered a very scientific exercise, as well as great fun. With training and experience, new heights and wonders can be achieved, and I am told there are organizations, exhibitions, gatherings of one sort or another, all dedicated to kite flying, with mutual inform- ation and support for like-minded owners—although I doubt whether my basic kite and its owner would be considered fit to join such a body. But no matter, I like it, I have it, and who knows what I might progress to next?

A word that has crept or catapulted into our vocabulary in recent years is 'ageism', an awareness that people may be discriminated against because of their age rather than who they are and what they are capable of doing. It certainly happens in many aspects of our life, and so maybe drawing attention to it, even passing legislation about it, could be a good thing. But perhaps it is up to older people themselves to combat the fallacies that direct what older people can or cannot do or enjoy. What is 'older' in one person's opinion can be quite young in another. Age can prove very elastic; it depends on how much 'give' there is, how much enthusiasm, energy, dedication and vision a person has.

As I read scripture I see how God chose and used people well past their prime to accomplish great deeds, attain new heights, win battles, inspire new hope and thought. What about Noah, Abraham and Sarah, Moses, Zechariah and Elizabeth, Simeon and Anna? Think how much we owe to John, who in his old age, exiled on the island of Patmos, saw and shared the great vision of what was to come. These were all people who were open to the Holy Spirit of God, and who allowed him to take them in new directions, filled with his power, showing the way for others to follow.

So often we know within us the calling of God. We feel him pulling, disturbing, inviting us to action, but we hold back, we offer our feeble excuses, we claim age exclusion, and so we miss out on the adventure of service, the joy of experiencing new life. A popular expression today is 'If you don't use it you lose it'—relating to physical ability, mental agility, even your cash in hand. It applies equally to spiritual capacity, to the endless opportunities we have, at any age, of discovering new truths and sharing them, achieving new heights of awareness of God's grace and power, and being enabled to inspire others, to draw them into a deeper fellowship with him. It is happening all the time, I see it and hear it. I know from personal experience just what the so-called older people are doing and being. I asked one man recently just how he came to be able to achieve so much for God at his age. His eyes twinkled as he said, 'Availability!'

What has all this to do with flying a kite? When I fly my kite, as I see it take to the air, as I feel the pull in my hand, the exhilaration in my heart, it is a reminder of the wind of the Spirit blowing over all creation, the wind of the Spirit of recreation, the wind of the Spirit who invites us to 'come fly with me', to be part of his work of touching lives, changing them, drawing them to the one who makes all things new— at any age or at any stage of life.

We are not told how old Zacchaeus was when he had that life-changing experience of meeting Jesus personally, and being welcomed by him as a friend. I imagine he was 'getting on'. After all, he was a chief tax-collector, and rich, obviously an astute businessman, although in a very unsavoury business. Despised and hated by his fellow Jews for being employed by the occupying power, he needed to watch his step, to be careful where he went and what he did. Not the sort of man you would expect to go shinning up a tree—but then he was desperate to see Jesus for himself. He was changed completely, in a moment, by

66

meeting with Jesus, and showed the evidence of the change by his practical response of generosity and restitution. It is often said that you cannot change the habits of a lifetime. Zacchaeus did! He 'flew a kite' by taking the invitation of Jesus with both hands. A free man with a whole new life, and a glorious future—and that can happen to anyone, anywhere, any time.

The 'wind of change' brings new life, breaking down the barriers of age, tradition and inclination. We too can only marvel and enjoy the freedom it gives, the energy it provides as it draws us onward and upward, new-born into the kingdom of heaven. Our date of birth, the tally of years, our physical age, have nothing to do with our spiritual life. The onset of greying hair, stiffening limbs, fading eyesight and hearing, the need for spare parts, pills and potions, holds no power over the spirit, and if we come to the point of even forgetting who we are, God never does, and never will. He keeps his promise: 'Behold, I make all things new.'

Are there kites in heaven? I sometimes wonder, as I fly my earthly one, feel the wind in my face, the tug of the line. But maybe the answer is, 'Fly now, know later'; and I look forward with eager anticipation to the glorious fulfilment of God's promise, living life to the full as part of his new creation for ever.

Jesus entered Jericho and was passing through it. A man was there named Zacchaeus; he was a chief tax-collector and was rich. He was trying to see who Jesus was, but on account of the crowd he could not, because he was short in stature. So he ran ahead and climbed a sycamore tree to see him, because he was going to pass that way. When Jesus came to the place, he looked up and said to him, 'Zacchaeus, hurry and come down, for I must stay at your house today.' So he hurried down and was happy to welcome him. All who saw it began to grumble and said, 'He has gone to be the guest of one who is a sinner.' Zacchaeus stood there and said to the Lord, 'Look, half of my possessions, Lord, I will give to the poor; and if I have defrauded anyone of anything, I will pay back four times as much.' Then Jesus said to him, 'Today salvation has come to this house, because he too is a son of Abraham. For the Son of Man came to seek out and to save the lost.'

Luke 19:1–10

Lord, the older I get the more inclined I am to think I know it all. I have gone through the 'been there, done it, seen it, got the T-shirt' stage, and now I just smile sweetly when any new suggestions are made, or changes are mooted; for I know, or I think I know, that there is nothing new under heaven. It has all been tried before, life goes round in circles, as others will realize when they get to my age and know what I know. It is a comfortable state to be in, very safe and secure. My layers of self-protection have been built up over the years, my views and opinions formed, almost cast in stone… and yet… suddenly I feel a pulling and tugging at my heart, my soul, as I open up, just a fraction. The wind rushes in, disturbing me, upsetting my carefully arranged life, turning things round, pushing me, inviting me, almost dancing with me, making me see beyond the safe and secure vista to a new horizon, and I know that is the place to be.

How can I leave all that I have accumulated so carefully, all that I have laboured over, built up with such care? I cannot begin again, not now; but then what is there here that I really need? How can I get there, beyond the horizon? What form of transport can I hail for the journey? The wind enfolds me, wrapping me into its embrace, and carries me up. Like a kite I fly, bursting with an energy not of my making or understanding. And now I know what it is to be truly myself, and truly part of you, released by the wind of your Spirit, yet held safe and secure by your hand of love and power. I am born again, reborn to share the new heaven and earth, part of your kingdom of renewed creation, of all things and all people made new. I am a child of your love through Jesus, brought home by your Spirit. Father, Son and Holy Spirit, I am made one with you—for ever.

And the one who was seated on the throne said, 'See, I am making all things new.'

Revelation 21:5

Chapter 14

TAKE YOUR
SHOES OFF

'Come in and have a coffee, Mum, I'm between clients.' My son had spotted me going past his office and invited me in. I was glad to put down my shopping and enjoy a break, and we sat together, happily chatting about life in general and nothing in particular. Then he sat back in his chair with a faraway look in his eyes and recounted an experience he had had after a night's fishing earlier in the week. 'I was just waking up, when I saw a flash of colour in front of me. It was a kingfisher. The mist was rising from the lake, the sun just appearing, and it was so beautiful. You couldn't buy a moment like that!'

We sat there in silence. He was reliving that moment of pure joy, and I was thanking God for the gift of a shared precious moment. It was something that was very special for him yet he had shared it with me, wanted me to enjoy it too. Then it was back to the business of the day, for him to get on with his work and for me to finish off my shopping and head for home.

Strangely enough—or not so strangely, for I believe God has a way of showing us his truth and beauty from many different angles, like a multi-faceted diamond—that same day I read an article by a member of the Society of the Love of God who had been to a conference in York. She wrote of her experience of being in York Minster, sitting in front of the great east window as the sun came up, and of the growing light illuminating the stained glass, and the wonder of 'being in the right place at the right time…'. I knew what she meant, for although I had not shared that particular moment I too have been caught up into experiences so beautiful, so awe-inspiring and so unexpected that although lasting for fleeting moments they remain for ever, providing strength and hope, a confidence that 'all shall be well' whatever the future may bring. I could identify with her feelings: 'as if everything—but really everything—was for the sake of each new moment, and anyone who, like myself, might wander in and taste it for the first time. It made nonsense of fears about the future.'

Only this week, after a particularly draining day of things that had to be done and demands for yet more, combined with trying to help someone in a desperately sad situation for which there seemed no way out, I went for a bicycle ride to give myself some space, time to clear my head and to try and make sense of a day that had so many question marks and jagged edges. It was late summer, and the fields were full of activity. Harvesting was in full flow, with harvesters and tractors followed by the flocks of birds, eager for their share of the golden grain. The dust was rising like smoke, the rattle of vehicles loud up and down those huge fields, anxious to 'get it in' before dusk. Even out here there seemed to be the same race against time.

I propped my cycle against a gate and stood looking across the fields at the sun, now sinking rapidly—and then came that very special moment when that huge ball of fire seemed to touch earth, and the sky, the earth turned a brilliant red, and a great stillness descended. Time came to a halt; eternity took over. The words that came into my mind at that moment were those that Moses heard as he looked into the burning bush at Horeb. 'Remove the sandals from your feet, for the place on which you are standing is holy ground.' I looked down at my own feet and smiled, for what was I wearing but a pair of old sandals? I did not take them off, but I got the message, the reminder of God's power and presence, and of the need for me to stand sill, to be still, not to race on, or in my case pedal on.

Julian, my fisherman son, has learned to sit and wait, so that he is in the right place at the right time to receive the gifts of the creator God. That member of the Society of the Love of God has, like so many others in religious orders, learned the value of sitting and waiting, of being in the right place at the right time. But most of us, and I include myself, often choose to be somewhere else doing something else, and we miss out. We are not there, so we lose out.

Moses had lived on a knife edge right from birth. He arrived in the world with a death sentence around his neck. The law of Pharaoh was, 'Every boy that is born to the Hebrews you shall throw into the Nile' (Exodus 1:22), but Moses, against all the odds, was saved by the ingenuity of his mother and sister, and the pity of Pharaoh's daughter. It was an odd upbringing, being the child of a Hebrew slave, but brought up as an Egyptian prince. It led to an identity crisis, the despair of being resented and rejected by his kinsfolk, having to run for his life, and exchange the lifestyle of a prince for that of a nomad shepherd. A new life, a safe one—that is, until he was curious enough to take a detour and examine a burning bush. Standing in the presence of God, hearing the voice of God, he received his authority for the seemingly impossible task of both rescuing his people, those who had rejected him, from the power of Pharaoh, and then leading them home as God's people, to the promised land.

God attracted Moses' attention through an experience of creation, and held him there by revealing himself: 'I am, who I am.' God still attracts our attention through his creation, and if we are wise we will look, listen, wait. We will take off our sandals, in a spiritual sense, by recognizing that we are in the presence of God, and giving him time to speak, to lead, to provide. Time only makes sense when seen in the light of eternity. Sadly, we are creatures of an instant society that only knows 'now', a fast-changing society that has no time to stop and take off the sandals of the mind, but is already racing on towards the horizon; and anything or anyone who would halt that rush is pushed aside, discarded. Yet if we will step aside, even though it is difficult to do so, then we will get life into perspective, a glimpse of the whole rather than being consumed by the immediate. For Moses, that stepping aside not only changed his own life, but the life of a nation, of society. He was entrusted to bring God's people out of slavery, not just from Egypt but from all that would hold them captive to sin and death, equipped with the blueprint of God's law, the making and living out of the covenant between God and his people.

A kingfisher across the water, the rising sun through stained glass, the setting sun on harvest fields, these are just instances of God's 'burning bushes' for 21st-century men and women who are willing to make time to look, to wonder and receive. Burning bushes come in all shapes and sizes, in all guises, and are often seen in unexpected places, but they remain God's invitation to us to draw near, to discover truth and purpose, and the strength and power to live it out in the light of time and eternity.

Moses was keeping the flock of his father-in-law Jethro, the priest of Midian; he led his flock beyond the wilderness and came to Horeb, the mountain of God. There the angel of the Lord appeared to him in a flame of fire out of a bush; he looked, and the bush was blazing, yet it was not consumed. Then Moses said, 'I must turn aside and look at this great sight, and see why the bush is not burned up.' When the Lord saw he had turned aside to see, God called to him out of the bush. 'Moses, Moses!' And he said, 'Here I am.' Then he said, 'Come no closer! Remove the sandals from your feet, for the place on which you are standing is holy ground.'
Exodus 3:1–5

Lord, sometimes I have a bit of a problem, a recurring problem which I put down to living in the fast lane of the first part of the 21st century. What it is, is tunnel vision. I can only see straight ahead; my feet and my head and heart will only go one way, forward. Everybody else around seems to be travelling the same road, so I join them, become part of the crowd. But every now and again I catch a glimpse of something to the side, over there, off the beaten track, and I find when I get near that I have to slow down, I want to sit down, I just want to be there. It is then that my vision clears, I can move my head, look up, around, and the view is quite different. It is wonderful, indescribably beautiful, quite perfect. There, at the centre of it all, you wait; you wait for me, you invite me to share in a vision of eternity, and I know I am on holy ground, in a holy place, for you are there. The tunnel clears, there's light at the end of it, and there along the way I see refreshment and renewal points, provision for my needs, help along the way. The invitations and the opportunities are there, at every stage; but sometimes I don't notice, I just rush by. It is my problem, my recurring problem, my tunnel vision restricting my view; so Lord, open my eyes. Open my eyes that I may see the way I should go, recognize your beauty, your love, your light, and glimpse your glory, both now, and fully in all eternity. Amen.

God said to Moses, 'I am, who I am… this is my name for ever, and this is my title for all generations.'
EXODUS 3:14–15

Chapter 15

MAN OF SORROWS

You may call me a pessimist or just well-organized, but I always like to give myself plenty of time to spare when travelling to meetings and appointments. It's perhaps because I was brought up by parents who were 'in service' and had their lives directed by the clock, but my father drilled into me that it was better to be an hour early than a minute late, and throughout my life I have found it a very good principle.

So it was in London, on a beautiful spring morning, that I found myself outside the building where I was to spend the day in meetings, over an hour early. Just nearby was Regent's Park and so, full of the joys of spring, I went into the park, congratulating myself on the opportunity to explore the exhibition of modern sculpture that was being held there, and to get plenty of fresh air to sustain me through a day which would be spent indoors. The large sculptures were scattered around the park, all biblical characters, and very impressive, and I quickened my pace so as to be able to see them all. As I turned a corner I came to a large sculpture of a man's head, his expression one of pain and anguish, of abandonment and desolation. The inscription read, 'Man of sorrows'. It was the face of Jesus Christ, and as I stood and looked at that face it was as though the stone cried out as he had done on the cross, 'My God, my God, why have you forsaken me?' I found myself unable to move. That face held me, those words thundered in my head almost as though I was hearing them for the very first time.

Then, as I turned to move on, I saw another man. He was lying on a park bench just behind the sculpture, curled up asleep. He had a couple of plastic bags as pillows, he was dirty and dishevelled, and his face bore the same expression as the carved stone which almost seemed to stand guard over him. Looking at these two faces, they were one and the same, 'man of sorrows', both at the very edge. I wondered whether to approach the sleeping man, and speak to him, or give him something. I took a step forward, then hesitated and drew back, whether from fear or compassion, I don't really know. He was deeply asleep, but even in sleep he had not been able to relax totally. Yet maybe in sleep he would be able to find some kind of escape and relief, so perhaps it was kinder to let him sleep, while he could, before he moved or was moved along.

I looked at my watch. There was still plenty of time to see the rest of the exhibition and I would return this way. If the man was awake, I would see if I could help him in any way, or at least I could give him the price of a meal. I walked on, but the exhibition had lost its appeal for me, and I soon made my way back to that park bench. I had taken some money from my bag and put it in my jacket pocket so I could easily slip it to him. I had rehearsed some words to say, some advice I would give him as to where he could go for help, but when I got to the bench it was empty. The man and his bags had gone. I felt guilty. I felt I had rejected him. I had had the opportunity, and had passed it by. As I looked at the sculpture, still standing guard over the bench, I saw the face of Christ and in it the face of the man who had lain on the bench—the face of suffering humanity, men and women, young and old, people in pain, mental, physical and spiritual, carrying such burdens, bearing such agony, crying out to God, 'Why have you forsaken me?', crying out to the passers-by, like me that morning, 'Why have you forsaken me?' and receiving no answer.

It was time for the day's business, the purpose of my visit to London. Up the steps, into the building, to be greeted warmly, the door opened for me. I walked into the conference room. Already some fellow members were there, talking, drinking coffee, shuffling papers, making notes. There were smiles and handshakes, a cup of coffee put into my hand, enquiries as to what sort of a journey I had had. We settled down around the big polished table, and prayed for God's blessing on our meeting, and for his guidance. I thought of the man in the park and prayed for God's blessing on him, and for guidance in his situation. And then we turned to the agenda, the reports, the facts and figures.

At the end of the day we all went our separate ways, back to our homes, our families, our friends, those who would welcome us, provide for us, those who loved us. Back to love, care, security, understanding. What about the man in the park? Where was he going that night, back to the park bench or another like it? Would anyone help him, listen to him, care for him? On the train home I opened my evening paper, to find so many stories of sadness, misery, violence, suffering and death, and I thought of that sculptured face of the 'Man of sorrows'—the face that said it all, for all time, the suffering face of man but also of God. I put the paper away, and looked out of the window, and at that very moment the sun broke through, evening sunshine flooding the passing scene with golden rays.

It was a kind of resurrection experience, somewhere between Peterborough and Newark, on a busy Great North Eastern Railway train. It was an experience of the 'Man of sorrows', but as he was three days later, the Living Lord, holding out his hands in greeting, 'Peace be with you', and offering his promise, 'I am with you always, even to the end of the age.' In him we recognize the promise fulfilled of redeemed, restored humanity, freed from mourning, crying, pain and death. Freed from the park benches of earth to a home in heaven.

I still think of the man on the bench in Regent's Park that morning. I wish I had spoken to him, done something for him, and that is something I have to live with. But the whole experience of that day has enabled me to take a small step forward in my understanding of what the incarnation is all about, of what it cost God to become flesh, and of the need for me to recognize him in others. I am no Mother Teresa, whose great love for God enabled her to be so close to her fellow human beings, whoever and whatever they were. I am Margaret Cundiff, marred, imperfect, weak, but I hope I am learning, by the grace of God, to recognize his image in others, to make the connection. Learning to look carefully with the heart as well as the eyes, to see what he wants me to see, and to respond.

He was despised and rejected by others;
a man of suffering and acquainted with infirmity;
and as one from whom others hide their faces,
he was despised, and we held him of no account.
Surely he has borne our infirmities
and carried our diseases;
yet we accounted him stricken,
struck down by God, and afflicted.
But he was wounded for our transgressions,
crushed for our iniquities;
upon him was the punishment that made us whole,
and by his bruises we are healed.

ISAIAH 53:3–5

Lord, suffering, pain and death: these are the great question marks that hang over our lives. When we see or experience these things we ask, 'Why?' and there seems to be no answer. Of course there are those who rationalize, philosophize and even spiritualize, and it looks so convincing put down on paper, or spoken from pulpit or rostrum; but not in the blood, the anguish and the tears when it comes home to us. 'Why?' is all we can cry out, in fear, in anger and despair.

Lord, you know, you understand, you have been there, for you too cried 'Why?'—you, the 'Man of sorrows'. You share in our suffering, our pain, our death. You hold us in your heart, and in your loving, healing presence we can find peace, comfort, assurance and life.

And I heard a loud voice from the throne saying, 'See, the home of God is among mortals. He will dwell with them; they will be his peoples, and God himself will be with them. He will wipe away every tear from their eyes. Death will be no more; mourning and crying and pain will be no more, for the first things have passed away.'

REVELATION 21:3–4

Chapter 16

CROSS, NOT CLOCK

It was such a peaceful spot, set back from the avenue of trees and surrounded by flowers. The small group of us stood together by the plot as I laid to rest the ashes of a friend from our village, alongside those of her husband and son. The simple service over, I left the rest of her family to say their own private goodbyes and walked up through the cemetery with the kindly official who had looked after the arrangements.

As we strolled back to the office together, I remarked how well everything looked, how beautifully cared for it all was. He smiled in appreciation and said, 'Yes, I enjoy my work, and I hope it helps people when they come here. We try to make it nice for them, to show that we respect their loved ones.' We walked on in silence, listening to the birds singing, breathing in the fragrance of the flowers. Then he remarked, 'I don't think I have seen you here before, have I?'

I explained that because my friend's husband and son were buried there, she had wanted to be put there with them, and I had come the distance to comply with her last wishes.

'Which church are you at then?' he asked, so I gave him a potted history of our church in Selby and then asked him about his work at the crematorium and cemetery. I discovered he had spent most of his working life there. Warming to my expression of interest, he began to point out to me some of the interesting and quite fascinating monuments and gravestones along our path, giving me a history lesson on some of the old worthies and families of an earlier age.

'You can learn a lot from inscriptions, can't you?' I commented.

'Yes you can, and they are all different, like you are.'

'Us?'

He nodded. 'Vicars, priests, ministers, you are all different, I meet all sorts here.'

I wondered what he had made of me!

'Well, it's like this. Some take their time, others rush the services through. There are those who are always last-minute, but then there are those who get it just right. They don't overrun, but they don't rush it either, and they always seem to have time for people, and know just what to say. You get to know them in this job.' He smiled. 'Did you know the vicar of…?' I shook my head. He went on, 'He was a lovely man; you could tell how much he cared for people, didn't rush them, before or after, he had time for everybody. Mind you, it didn't always suit. I always remember when one chap complained he took up too much time, and do you know what he did? He just put his arm round that man's shoulder, took him back into the chapel, pointed up and said, "See that? It's a cross, not a clock." He didn't say anything else, but he had made his point, and it was taken. I've always remembered that.'

I glanced behind me and saw the family were coming along, so I stopped and shook hands with my companion. 'Thank you for telling me that, I'll remember it too.' With that we parted, he back into his office, and me to rejoin the family and to make our journey back to Selby.

I often think of that conversation we had in Leeds, and of the story of the vicar who had made such an impression on him. I am grateful that he shared it with me. There are some things that stick in the mind. In fact, they do more than that, they penetrate the heart. They are seeds of loving wisdom gathered from the depths of experience and under-standing, which can take root and flower in the lives of others, and bring forth fruit far beyond the original planting. They influence our thinking, our attitude and actions. Sometimes when I want to hurry a situation along, when someone is going over the same old ground, over and over again; when I am caught and held up by the person who goes on and on, and I find I am beginning to feel irritated or weary, anxious to get away; then I try to remember those words, 'It's a cross, not a clock.' I try to forget the watch on my wrist, the clock on the wall, and remember the one who died on the cross out of love for me and for the one beside me from whom I am trying to escape. I would like to say it changes my attitude. Sadly, it doesn't always, but sometimes it does, and I am grateful it has, for so often I have then been able to see beyond the obvious to the real issue confronting the person beside me or on the other end of the phone. A few extra minutes of time and attention has made all the difference for someone struggling to explain how they really felt, what was in their heart to say.

So much is said today about giving others 'quality time', which means concentrating wholly on the other person, rather than allowing other things to intrude upon that space. I applaud that, but it can be something of an excuse to say, 'Well, I can only give him/her a short amount of my time, but I give them quality time', when what might be needed is an open-ended relationship, a relaxation of schedule, based on love for that other person—the love that does not count the cost or the clock, but provides all that is needed, and more besides. Remember what Jesus said about going the second mile? 'If anyone forces you to go one mile, go also the second mile' (Matthew 6:41)—which can be interpreted in time as well as distance, time given graciously and voluntarily, rather than grudgingly and under pressure. Under these conditions we may find ourselves discovering hidden reserves of grace and strength which will take us even further along our path of obedience and love, following in the steps of our Lord and Saviour, Jesus Christ.

'Give and it will be given to you. A good measure, pressed down, shaken together, running over, will be put into your lap; for the measure you give will be the measure you get back.'
LUKE 6:38

80

Lord, I have to confess that sometimes I have my eyes on the clock rather than on you and your love. I dole out what I call 'my time' in small measure, making sure I do not waste it, forgetting you spared no love's expense to ensure for me an eternal future, and that you have bidden me share your love, whatever it costs me, with others. When I do look away from myself, and my preoccupation with the passing of time, I am freed to love and to serve you, and enabled to open my arms and my heart to others too, to enjoy the freedom that your love gives. You give in full measure, your love overflows, renewing, restoring, drawing me ever closer to you, opening up the joys of eternity. Grant me the grace to know and live within it, and reflect it in the time you have given me here on earth.

Jesus said, 'This is my commandment, that you love one another as I have loved you. No one has greater love than this, to lay down one's life for one's friends. You are my friends if you do what I command you… I am giving you these commands so that you may love one another.'
JOHN 15:12–14, 17

Chapter 17

ON THE EIGHTH
DAY

I was surprised, intrigued and maybe even a little flattered to receive
an invitation to a 'working lunch' to discuss the issues raised by the
Review of the See of Canterbury. Up to then I had never given the
matter any thought, apart from feeling that the role of the Archbishop
of Canterbury, in fact of any archbishop, was an impossible task for
any one person. It is composed of so many different facets, and to meet
the expectations of so many varying divisions internationally and
nationally, of Church and State, would challenge even an archangel,
never mind an archbishop. I agreed, perhaps more out of curiosity than
anything else, and so found myself on a late autumn day along with
four other clergy from the York diocese heeding the instruction of the
chairman to 'sit where you like as long as we can see your faces', which
sounded to me slightly ominous.

As we took our seats for lunch, other members of the review team
were interspersed between us, we were formally introduced, and so the
process began. I could well understand why the members of the review
team had been chosen, and I could also see why my four fellow
members from the diocese had. The only question was, why had I been
included? I still do not know, but I did find that working lunch hour
an interesting exercise, not for anything I may have contributed, but for
the exchange of views, the way in which ideas were listened to, the
concern for the future role of the Archbishop of Canterbury, to enable
whoever has the responsibility of that office to be able to fulfil it. What
warmed my heart was the evident desire not just to get the job

specification right, but to make sure the right support, of every kind, was put in place. The role has changed, and will continue to change; and as Jesus reminded the people of his day new wine cannot be put into old wineskins. In our 'new wine' society, old structures are not able to contain the sheer volume of demand, without breaking down and so losing what is precious and necessary. In the Church, as well as in every part of society, we have to move forward, using the expertise of today as well as the experience of yesterday.

My contribution to such a major issue was a very minor one, and there will have been many such consultations taking place, but I appreciated that glimpse into the process, which sparked within me questions which maybe I would never have considered before that day. One of the seemingly offbeat questions thrown into our discussion was, 'What if there was an extra day within the week, an eighth day? What could be put into it that at the moment is not possible?'

My unspoken first reaction to that was to consider it a ridiculous question. After all, God created the world in six days, and rested on the seventh. He is not likely to amend that for our benefit. It took a while for me to grasp the implications of that seemingly silly question. As I went straight from the lunch table to rush round the local supermarket to ensure our table for the week was provided for, and then dashed to the crematorium to say a last goodbye to an old friend, and later drove back home before a meeting that evening, I thought hard and long about that eighth day. Not in regard to the work load of the Archbishop of Canterbury, but to my own lifestyle. What essential parts of my life were unattended to because I had filled up, not only six days, but seven, with the less important? If I had another day, clear, free, untouched, what and who should be given that space?

It was, I found, a painful process, and very revealing, and it was nothing to do with meetings, organizations, discussions, activities at all. It was to do with my relationship with God, the God I claimed to love and serve, the God who had given me life, and new life, the God who I proudly said was first in every part of my life, who received priority over everything and everyone else. Was he just an eighth-day God, while I blithely sang, 'Seven whole days, not one in seven I will

83

praise thee'. Had he been squeezed out, given just the tail end of what was left in each day? Yes, I spent so much time *for* him, but what about *with* him? But then, if there were to be an eighth day I could give him it all, couldn't I? I knew well enough what my order of priority should be, must be, and I knew too that I had seven days a week already given by God, to use wisely and aright. Get the priority right, the rest would flow—then there would be enough time.

God is merciful and compassionate, and I believe he has a sense of humour, for every now and again he breaks the mould, and gives me an extra special gift of time. Perhaps he does have an eighth day up his sleeve for special occasions, when he knows I really do desperately need one, and that without it I am in danger of running to waste out of my constricting self-made old wineskin. A day suddenly appears, cleared as by an unseen but knowing hand. A meeting is cancelled, the train service is out of operation, an expected situation does not materialize, and my programme vanishes into thin air, leaving time and space, with love from God to me, and we enjoy it together. Just being alone with God, sitting on the seat in the garden, walking down the lane, in the quiet of the sanctuary in church, or with my feet up at home—such times leave me refreshed, relaxed, renewed, and I always say the same thing: 'I should do this more often!' I am sure God smiles, because he has heard it all before; but as I say, he is merciful and compassionate, and very understanding. He gives me that eighth day just to prove to me that seven days are enough, but if I get desperate he can make an eighth day out of seven, and so can I if I really want to, really need to. The way it is done is by freeing up one of the seven, and giving it, sharing it, with God, who created me and all the world, and who sustains everything by his love and power, in his way, in his time, and for good.

Looking back at that unexpected invitation to a working lunch I am thankful that I was included, for whatever reason. I am grateful for that strange-sounding question, and for what I gained from pondering it. Who knows, one day an archbishop might say to me, 'Margaret, if there was an eighth day in the week, what do you think I should put in it?' But then, if he is wise, he will have discovered the answer already, and put it into practice. He will just be making sure I am doing the same!

God saw everything that he had made, and indeed, it was very good. And there was evening and there was morning, the sixth day. Thus the heavens and the earth were finished, and all their multitude. And on the seventh day God finished the work that he had done, and he rested on the seventh day from all the work that he had done. So God blessed the seventh day and hallowed it, because on it God rested from all the work that he had done in creation.

GENESIS 1:31—2:3

Father, you created the world and everything in it in six days, and still had time to spare. You modelled a measured division of life, perfectly spaced, with no rush, recognized its order and beauty, and then had a day to rest, to enjoy it. I know, of course, that days with you are not as with us, but you fulfilled all that was needed in perfect order, then gave us your master plan to live by— six days to work, a day to rest, a regular pattern. Day and night, work and rest, praise and worship, just like breathing, steady, renewing heart, mind and spirit.

It worked well, for generation upon generation; but then we began to get impatient. We wanted more out of life, to put more into it, and the days were not enough for all we wanted to cram into them. So we took the seventh day and made it like the other six. Now we will have more time, we thought, for ourselves; but somehow it still was not enough. If only we had another day, then... tempers frayed, we got stressed, life became drudgery, the joy was squeezed out of it. We had poured too much into the days, stretched the fabric of life until it began to burst, collapse, decay. No time, no inclination to praise, to worship, to rest, to be—and who was to blame? But if there was an eighth day then...

We are silly children at times. We go beyond our limits and wonder why we are hurting, why we cannot find our way. But you are a merciful, loving Father, and you reach out and hold us, still us, revive us, bring us back into the rhythm of your love, day and night, work and rest, praise and worship. You give me not another day, but another chance, to learn to let go of our timed agenda and find our peace in your eternal plan. For you are Alpha and Omega, the beginning and the end. You offer us life in all its fullness, and for this we give you our unending thanks and praise.

Jesus said, 'So do not worry about tomorrow, for tomorrow will bring worries of its own. Today's trouble is enough for today.'
MATTHEW 6:34

Chapter 18

COME AND SEE

From its very beginning I was captivated by the prospect of the Millennium Dome. I felt excited about this great tented palace of multivaried experiences, and avidly followed the story of its design and building. I remember seeing it in its early stages as it began to take shape, something so different on the London skyline that, whatever anyone thought, it could not be ignored. I followed its progress through the media reports and special programmes, and was alarmed by the chaos, arguments, and lack of any common strategy. Cash, or the lack of it, raised its menacing head, and bitter wrangling and recriminations followed it all the way. While I recognized that there were great problems, I could also see that there was enthusiasm and vision, coupled with 'hands on' determination to make it a success, in spite of all the sniping that went on from so many quarters. The opening ceremony was marred, not just by teething troubles but by the attitude of some of those who had made up their mind long ago that it would not be a success. Reports were not encouraging, and so the general public voted with its feet. Numbers were down, costs went up, and the rest, as they say, is history.

I read, I watched, I listened to the varying reports as the year un-folded, and was still determined to see it for myself. For the most part, when I mentioned that I intended to visit the Dome I got surprised looks, teasing comments from 'Surely you don't want to waste your money on that... I wouldn't have thought it was your sort of thing...' to the rather condescending 'But haven't you heard...?' as though I was quite unaware of all that was going on. As someone who was around for, and enjoyed, the Festival of Britain nearly fifty years previously, I am made of sterner stuff than some people would give me credit for, and nothing was going to stop me finding out for myself and making up my own mind about the Millennium Dome.

So it was on a cold, dry day in spring that I entered that great arena, into my millennium experience. From the first moment I felt like a child again, excited, curious, eager to see and try everything. My daughter, abandoning any hope of keeping me in check, could only remark, 'You like this, don't you, Mother?' as I flew round the zones, ready for anything and everything. Settling back for the Millennium Show I was transported into a wonderful land of colour and sound, delighting in that extraordinary spectacle of dance, drama and aerial performance, seeing the young performers putting everything they had into making it an experience of a lifetime.

Eventually, and reluctantly, we left. It was closing time, and our visit had seemed only a few minutes, but what minutes they were! I had been, I had experienced it for myself, and I had loved it, and will always remember it. On 31 December 2000 the Dome closed. The year was over and it was finished for ever. I have my memories, the book, the photographs, and I was there! No one can ever take it away from me; but as for those who never made the trip, they lost their opportunity. The records will stand, the reports will be available, the discussions will go on. Let them, I say. I made up my own mind based on my own experience, not on hearsay. It is the only way to really know, to have a basis for judgment. All the rest is second-hand.

I cannot help thinking of the shepherds on the hillside on the first Christmas night. They could have been forgiven for thinking the lights, the music, the voice of an angel, were an illusion, some strange phenomenon, but they had the sense to say, 'Let us go and see...'. The star in the east might have provided great material for philosophical discussion, but the wise men were prepared to follow it, to find out for themselves. The fishermen were willing to leave their boats and follow Jesus, the tax-collector his livelihood, to discover a new life. Nathanael responded to the challenge of Philip to 'come and see', to find and to follow. The crowds were not content just to hear about Jesus but were willing to follow him, mile after mile, without thought of food or drink, so as to see and hear him for themselves. The Greeks made a special journey in the hope of meeting Jesus, coming to ask Philip, 'Sir, we would see Jesus.' We only have to read the Gospel accounts to discover the lengths people would go to meet Jesus face to face, to be in his presence, to hear his voice, to witness his works of mercy.

There were those who met Jesus for themselves and decided he was not for them. They could not accept him, they disagreed with all he stood for, and some found what he demanded of them too great: 'This teaching is difficult; who can accept it?' and 'Because of this many of his disciples turned back, and no longer went about with him' (John 6:60, 66). There was the young man so desperate to be with Jesus that he came running to him, kneeling before him, but when he was told what it would cost him he turned away, sad, but unable to pay the price of discipleship. But both for those who came and stayed and for those who went away, they had made a personal journey, and based on that experience they made their decision. Jesus did not force anyone to follow him, but offered the choice, setting out clearly and plainly what it meant. Then it was up to them to decide for themselves, yes or no.

For two thousand years the message has been, 'Come and see', the invitation has been to meet with Jesus, to realize what he offers, to understand what acceptance implies. He does not play games, or water down his message, or hide the cost with sugary sentiment. We cannot choose observer status and be truly his disciple, nor can we sit between two opinions according to the fads and fashions of the age. When I was trying to explain this to a friend recently, my friend said impatiently, 'The trouble with you is that you are too black and white. There is no room for grey, and most of life is a varying shade of grey.' I agreed with her. There are many grey areas in life, and we have to decide whether we choose a whiter shade or darker shade, and the result is very much the same; but not with Jesus! 'No one can serve two masters, for a slave will either hate the one and love the other, or be devoted to the one and despise the other. You cannot serve God and wealth.' Who said that? Jesus. Take a look at Matthew 6:24, and perhaps, while you have the passage open, read through the whole of chapters 5 to 8, what is known as 'The Sermon on the Mount', and decide whether it offers a choice of black or white, or a varying shade of grey.

Most people find Jesus interesting. He excites curiosity, there is something about him that commands attention, but many shrink away from getting too personal, from allowing him to infiltrate their space. He is a good talking point, his teaching fascinates and the concept of his rising from the dead will always provoke an argument, so long as he is kept at arm's length, locked away in a book or a building. Jesus does not invite discussion or debate, but gives a personal invitation to meet him. He promises that if you really mean business, if you would meet with him, he is there waiting, right beside you. All he asks is that you listen, you trust him, you give yourself time to attune your heart and mind to him. Sometimes it will be a sudden revelation, or maybe just a gentle growing awareness of his presence, but he is there, no doubt about that, because he always keeps his promise. What happens next is for you to decide.

The next day Jesus decided to go to Galilee. He found Philip and said to him, 'Follow me.' Now Philip was from Bethsaida, the city of Andrew and Peter. Philip found Nathanael and said to him, 'We have found him about whom Moses in the law and also the prophets wrote, Jesus, son of Joseph from Nazareth.' Nathanael said to him, 'Can anything good come out of Nazareth?' Philip said to him, 'Come and see.'
JOHN 2:43–46

Lord Jesus Christ, two thousand years ago you walked this earth, you made God real to men and women of your day, you showed his love and his power, through your teaching and preaching, through miracles of healing, and acts of compassion and mercy. You showed them how to live, and how to die. You offered them a new life, your life, for ever. It was a very different world from our world of today, two thousand years on, and yet through the years, the centuries, you have remained the same, offering your friendship, your love, and your power to live your life; for you not only lived and died, but rose again, and you are here for us, men and women of a new millennium that bears witness to you. You are here, friend and Saviour, Lord and God, King of Kings, of earth and heaven. You invite us to come to you, to meet you, to become part of you, here and now. You say to us 'Come and see, come to me', to feel your touch upon our lives that brings forgiveness and healing, strength and hope. You are here, and all we need to do is say 'Yes', now.

'O Lamb of God, I come.'

'I had heard of you by the hearing of the ear, but now my eye sees you.'
JOB 42:5

Chapter 19

WHO AM I?

I had known Joan for years. She was an active member of a local church and of various organizations in the town, and we were always bumping into one another and enjoyed stopping for a chat. A lively, cheerful lady in her mid-sixties, she had been widowed a few years previously, but had a married son and daughter living in the area, and now, much to her delight, she had become a grandmother for the first time. We met as she was coming out of Boots and I was going in.

'Would you like to see the baby?' she said, and brought out the photographs she had just collected. Her eyes were shining as she passed the pictures over: 'Here she is, a day old. This is her with her mum and dad… this is her other gran and grandad, and our Peter and his wife, and here's one with me…'.

'She's a lovely baby, she has a look of you, I can see you in her,' I said.

'Oh go on, you can't,' she protested, but I could see she was pleased.

We stood for a few more minutes together and then rather hesitantly she said, 'Would you pop in to see me sometime? I'd like to talk to you.' I could tell by her tone it was something important, so I got out my diary and we fixed it there and then.

As we sat together in her home later that week I could see she was anxious, and so I gently said, 'Now, something is worrying you. What is it?'

At that she burst into tears, and sobbed and sobbed. I thought for a moment something was wrong with her grandchild. 'Is it the baby?' I asked.

She shook her head. 'It's me, I don't know who I am.'

Then she poured out her story. She had been adopted as a baby, but had not found out until after her parents had died, discovering the adoption papers in their effects. It had come as a profound shock to her, but she had never told anyone, pushing it away to the back of her mind. The birth of her granddaughter had triggered the memory and now she did not know how to handle the knowledge she had.

'Do you really want to know?' I asked her. She nodded. 'Well, let's see what you can find out. Here's what you will need to do.' I gave her some practical advice on how to begin the process, then we sat together and prayed that whatever was best would be revealed, and that she would be able to accept it. As I left her I said, 'And now enjoy being a granny!'

It took quite some time before Joan was able to discover more about her natural parents. Her mother had been very young, her father a soldier, never heard of again. It had been one of those wartime romances, and she had been the result. All attempts to find her mother proved fruitless, and as Joan says, 'She is probably dead now, but I would have liked to have known her, for my children to have known their grandmother, for her to have had the pleasure I have from my granddaughter.' Not a happy ending to the story, but the sharing of her problem, and doing all she could to find out more, helped Joan, and gradually she has come to accept the situation, thankful for her adoptive parents, and respecting their action in keeping the facts from her as being out of love for her. As she says, 'They couldn't have been better parents to me. They gave me everything they could, but I would have liked to have known.'

Joan's story is not unique, I hear many such accounts, particularly from men and women of that particular age group, now in their fifties and sixties, and many of them have begun the search for their natural parents, brothers and sisters. Some, like Joan, had not found out they were adopted until after the death of their adoptive parents. Others, having been told, have waited out of love until the death of those who have loved and cared for them, so as not to hurt them. Nowadays there are many agencies willing to help people find their natural parents and families, and in this modern age there are so many means of doing so, not least through the media. There are many happy endings; but it is also a very dangerous business, and rejection can and does prove doubly hurtful when contact is refused, for various reasons. It is something that has to be entered into very sensitively, with awareness of the problems it may throw up.

Going through this with Joan, I came to realize that the issue is even bigger than wanting to find a parent or family. It is to do with roots, belonging, identity. Joan still often says to me, 'If only I had a photograph, a letter, just something. My past is a blank sheet of paper, and I feel incomplete, even though I have children and grandchildren. There is part of me I long to know, and I never will now.' Most people have that longing to know, to find out their roots, and classes on genealogy, 'tracing your family tree', have proved very popular.

My husband Peter and his cousin have gone to endless trouble tracing the Cundiff family tree, and what an interesting story it tells! Certainly there are some skeletons in the cupboard, but they have proved to be quite exciting, adding a deal of spice to the tale. I greatly value a series of photographs of my mother's family, dating back several generations, which she carefully labelled while she was alive so I would have the benefit of seeing my forebears, and it is fascinating to see family likenesses passing down through the generations. West Country born, I find a great affinity with the area where my mother's family lived for generations, a sense of history, belonging, being part of it all, and so I can appreciate the sadness of those who have no such store to delve into and enjoy.

But what will the words 'family', 'roots', 'belonging', mean to third-millennium men and women, if anything? We are seeing the continuing breakdown of family life, the disintegration of close-knit structures. Families and friends are scattered throughout the world, no longer living next door or in a nearby village or town. We may proudly claim to be a global village, but it is a village of independent individuals, isolated, immune. All the technology is in place to bring it together, but the heart seems to be missing. The drawstrings of affection, love, common concern to connect with each other have been discarded in favour of anonymous microchips. We face a lost world of aimless people crying in the wilderness, 'Who am I?' and receiving no answer. It's a frightening prospect, but we need to be aware of it, and act before it is too late, before we lose sight of where we came from, who we are, and our eternal destiny.

God's plan for all creation from the beginning was that we would not live in isolation, but together, in families and communities, enabling one another to live fulfilled and productive lives. As God looked at Adam, the man he had made for fellowship with him, he said, 'It is not good that the man should be alone; I will make him a helper as his partner' (Genesis 2:18). Family life was to be the framework of society. The extended family was the norm, including the poor and needy, the strangers and travellers, and throughout the Bible we are reminded that this is God's command to all of us, that even the lost, those who stray, are to be sought and brought back, given the opportunity to be restored within the family. Jesus' mission was to bring back the lost, and we have those compelling pictures in the parables of the lost coin, the lost sheep, the lost son, of everything and everyone being valuable, needed, and worth saving. We must never lose sight of that, whatever happens in society. The Church must be committed to God's ideal of family life, to everyone having a place and part.

We say the Church is a family, and so it is, but we cannot afford to leave it there. It demands our constant attention, our reaching out to others to bring them in. Not to fill up the pews, or boost the weekly collection, but to enjoy their place as honoured family members. The Mothers' Union keeps this in the forefront of its aims—'to promote conditions in society favourable to stable family life, and the protection of children', and 'to help those whose family life has met with adversity' (two of its five objectives)—and those aims are lived out and worked out imaginatively and practically by its members in all areas of the Church and society, in this country and overseas—and, of course, by many other organizations and agencies committed to this vital ministry.

'The family' is an expression often trotted out to make political capital, and heads are nodded in agreement about the need to support family life. But to sustain family life, to encourage the extended family across the frontiers, needs more than votes, nods and raised hands. It is a matter of heart, will and action, and we need to act now, while we have the opportunity; now, while there is still time.

Can a woman forget her nursing child,
or show no compassion for the child of her womb?
Even these may forget,
yet I will not forget you.
See, I have inscribed you on the palms of my hands.
ISAIAH 49:15–16

Father, you hold out your hands in love and understanding to all people. No one is beyond your knowledge or compassion. Each name is written on your hands, on your heart, each equally welcomed, wanted, known.

We look out on a world where so many are nameless, unknown and unloved, isolated, lost and alone. Enable us, by your love, to open our hands and heart, giving and caring, understanding and welcoming, that together we may realize the joy of being your family, here on earth, until that time when we are all gathered together in your eternal home, to your praise and glory.

Father of orphans and protector of widows
is God in his holy habitation.
God gives the desolate a home to live in;
he leads out the prisoners to prosperity.
PSALM 68:5–6

Chapter 20

THE JOY THAT KNOWS NO ENDING

We had thought hard and long about it, examined the brochures, and our bank accounts, talked to those who had been there, and to the travel agent who spelt out all the details. We read the books and watched the video, and then we booked it, to celebrate our fortieth wedding anniversary. The 'world's most beautiful voyage', it was called, the Norwegian coastal journey from Bergen to the North Cape. Our forty years of marriage would not be marked with 'things', but graced with the joy of discovery, we decided.

The days running up to our departure were crowded, busy, enjoyable. The delight of a celebration meal with the family at an old country house, the fun of celebrating with the church family after the Sunday morning service, the 'open house' days which we shared with friends and neighbours in our own home; the comings and goings and the fulfilment of engagements, tying up the loose ends, and even trying to clear my desk, or at least part of it. Then at last the excitement of walking up the gangway of the ship and being welcomed aboard—now the journey had really begun. The next few hours passed in a dream of exploring our surroundings, gathering information, enjoying a meal; and then tiredness overcame us, and we fell into our beds with a prayer of thanksgiving and a sleepy goodnight.

It was the sun streaming in that woke me. I lay, trying to work out where I was, and then I remembered! I sat up and looked out of the cabin window to see the most amazing scene. We were gliding along, almost noiselessly, past small islands, the snow-covered mountains coming right down to the shore, and the sun already high in the sky, bathing everything in a golden glow. I sat enchanted by the wonder of it all, hardly daring to breathe in case I disturbed it. Peter slept on, oblivious, so I woke him. 'Look, you are missing it all!' Together we sat, just gazing at the passing scene, unable to speak, overcome with its beauty.

Eventually I asked, 'What time is it?'

Peter looked at his watch, 'A quarter to three! Back to sleep!' I had forgotten we were in the land of the midnight sun in midsummer!

As I tried to get back to sleep I remembered how as a child I had woken very early one Christmas morning, even earlier than a quarter to three, and had opened my Christmas presents, with loud whoops of delight—'He has been!'—until my parents had put me firmly back to bed again, ordering me, 'Go to sleep, or else.' Now it was Christmas all over again, in midsummer and sixty-odd years later. The same delight, the same exhilaration, the same sense of awe and fulfilment.

During the next few days we experienced so many new things: fjords and flowers, reindeer and sea eagles, waterfalls cascading down, the majestic glacier. Each port of call was a new experience, giving a glimpse of a completely new way of life. There was the marvel at crossing the Arctic Circle, that invisible line, or standing at the North Cape gazing, it seemed, into eternity; and all in company with fellow travellers, strangers who became friends, bonded together in the joy of discovery.

But as they say, 'all good things come to an end' and it was soon back to the daily routine of life, the familiar, well-trodden paths, but with the memories, the photographs and so many reminders of a special journey. But memories can never quite give that same tingle of excitement and wonder as when we first opened our eyes and ourselves to the experience.

I often wonder how John felt on the Isle of Patmos during his long exile, following his view through that open door into heaven (Revelation 4:1). Did the vision fade with time? Did he ever wonder if he had imagined it rather than experienced it? The description which has come down to us through this last book of the New Testament is crystal clear. It has an immediacy, a power that allows us into the very presence of God. It is no earthly journey that fades with time, but an ever-new revelation of eternity. It is outside time as we know it, and a foretaste of heaven. We glimpse 'all things new', and a continuous experience of the new life prepared for God's people. For John, I am sure, the vision never faded, the joy never ended, and now, with all God's children in heaven, he rejoices in discovering all things new, continuously, because the life of God never ends. It is not a static state but a continuing journey.

It is difficult for us to begin to imagine just what that means, we who are so controlled by time, confined within its limits, driven by the clock. I am sure that in heaven there will be no watches or clocks. They will have no place of purpose, but like all the other restraints of earth they will have passed away, along with the rest of the clattering, chattering toys and torments of a weary old world—the misunderstandings, the half-understood opportunities, the tears, the fears, the pains and losses. Evil, sin and death will no longer have any power over us, will no longer be able to hurt or hinder us, for they have been dealt with, defeated, and we are freed from their power by the love of Jesus. He died for us, and he has redeemed us, given us entrance into new life. It is ours to enjoy, to live, to grow in.

When we pass through the open door into heaven we will be truly ourselves, as God intended we should be. To 'rest in the Lord' is not a state of inactivity, but the time to enjoy the glorious freedom of the knowledge of God, to serve and praise and worship with 'all the company of heaven'. It is a constant and continuing state of discovering all that God has prepared for us, which will never come to an end. Here on earth we have our 'cut-off points'. Even the most perfect holidays come to an end, successes and pleasures evaporate; we grow tired and weary, our senses blunted and deadened, our minds and bodies weakened. We do not have the capacity or inclination to keep on attempting new challenges and aspirations. We are mortal, limited, and as the psalmist reminds us, 'our years come to an end like a sigh' (Psalm 90:9). Yet within us is the seed of new life, which God brings to fruition as we pass from death to life. No longer will we have the restrictions of time, of earth, but instead the realization of our inheritance of the kingdom of heaven, and the divine energy to enjoy it. God is still at work in his kingdom making all things new, and we will share with him the glory of it.

And the one who was seated on the throne said, 'See, I am making all things new.' Also he said, 'Write this, for these words are trustworthy and true.' Then he said to me, 'It is done! I am the Alpha and the Omega, the beginning and the end. To the thirsty I will give water as a gift from the spring of the water of life. Those who conquer will inherit these things, and I will be their God and they will be my children.'
REVELATION 21:5–7

Lord, thank you for the joys of earth, for the gift of the world around us, and for the capacity to discover, to wonder, to be excited, to be filled with awe and anticipation. You enable us to have foretastes of heaven, glimpses of eternity, to reach out and know your presence, made manifest in creation. You are the God of surprises; you delight to amaze and mystify us, reminding us of your power and your love, allowing us to taste and see your goodness, to sample the joys of eternity, before the day when we will enter into that new heaven and new earth, and be at home with you—for ever.

Jesus said, 'Do not be afraid, little flock, for it is your Father's good pleasure to give you the kingdom.'
LUKE 12:32

Chapter 21

WHAT SORT OF
A GOD?

It was one of those perfect summer mornings. The sun was high in the sky, with just a hint of a breeze to ruffle the leaves of the trees and to set the flowers nodding beside the path. The old church looked a picture, standing there as it had done for hundreds of years, the sunshine lighting up the stonework with fingers of gold.

There was the buzz of conversation as the congregation started coming out of church, the children racing out ahead, some of the older people gathered in little knots, exchanging news and greetings, and murmurs of 'lovely day, nice to see you, good to be here…'. I stood outside the porch shaking hands, enjoying the warmth of the sun and of friendship, refreshed by sharing in worship, thankful for the privilege of ministry—a sort of 'God's in his heaven, all's right with the world' feeling, and a sense of satisfaction in being part of it all.

A man took my hand and held it, commanding my attention. He was smiling, but his eyes were steely and his posture confrontational. 'I don't recognize that God you were talking about this morning,' he said, quietly, but very distinctly. 'That powerful, all-knowing, all-loving God of yours. If he does exist, then he has got quite a bit of explaining to do.'

I raised my eyebrows and invited, 'Tell me.'

He proceeded to tell me in no uncertain terms, quoting several incidents from the Old Testament when it was reported that God wiped out nations and peoples, where he used them as examples of the fate that awaited wrongdoers, where innocent people were slaughtered so that God's people might go forward.

My feeble attempt to try to explain that this was history as seen through the people of the day only caused him to snort, 'I thought you said it was God's word. Now you change your tune!' Then he seemed to relax: 'I'm not getting at you personally, I just want to know who this God is.'

I tried to point him to those words of Jesus, 'He who has seen me has seen the Father', to remind him of the love shown to us in his life, death and rising again, of the promise of forgiveness, power and hope for all who would put their trust in him. He looked at me and said coldly, 'Don't you ever look at the world around you, at what is going on? Do you ever read the papers or listen to the news, or do you live in there?' He gestured towards the church. 'You should get out more,' and with that he strode off.

I drove home feeling rather chastened, and ineffective. The man had touched me on some raw issues, but on one major point he was wrong. I do live in the real world, I am aware of the problems, and I am confronted with madness, suffering and pain, with anger, frustration and fear, day by day; not just 'out there' but in the lives of those I meet with in many differing situations. But I have no easy answers; in fact, in many cases I have no answer, no consolation, for these things do not make sense nor can they be explained away. I do believe God is all-powerful, all-knowing and all-loving. I know that he has shown and does show himself through Jesus Christ. I am also aware, and know by personal experience, that evil, suffering, pain, injustice, failure, death and destruction are rampant in our world, as they always have been.

Power, knowledge and love should be able to cancel out all that hurts and harms created life; and if God is the creator and sustainer, then why doesn't he intervene? If the cross was the victory over pain and death, why do people still suffer horrendous pain, dying in agony, when the Christian gospel claims to be the answer? We hear of thousands upon thousands dying of starvation through famine and drought in one part of Africa, and in another through floods, disease, and conflict. In India, the Middle East and Europe, wars and disputes continue to escalate, the innocent paying the biggest price, caught up in issues they neither

102

know about nor are concerned with. Diseases take their toll, defeating the best of medical and surgical care and skill. Children are still born terribly handicapped, young people are cut off in their prime, the accident rates soar, crime stalks the streets, relationships are broken, hearts are wounded and scarred, the weary and depressed find no solace or way out. A sorry picture? Yes it is, and so I can sympathize with that man's expression of anger against a God whom he despises and rejects. Yesterday a young mother came to me in tears asking for prayer for a friend, another young mother with two small children, who has been diagnosed with inoperable cancer. At the same time I heard of an accident where a young mother was killed in a car crash with her eighteen-month-old son, and of a father of two teenaged children killed by a hit-and-run driver.

I am not surprised when people question a loving God, and yet it is equally true that courage, love, patience and faith flourish even in and through such situations. I think of the man I met in town today who has cared for an invalid wife for eighteen years. She needs his attention 24 hours a day and he gives it lovingly and without complaint. 'I'll never give up on her,' he said. A letter received today from an elderly friend, now in a nursing home, says, 'I am fairly well, dear Violet not so. We are both in the above home, but Violet does not know me. Her memory has gone, but we are together which is all that matters. God has helped us to achieve our diamond wedding.' I have just finished reading a report from one of the mission agencies working in some of the worst areas in the world, amid dangers and deprivation, and they give instance after instance of the joy of young volunteers, doctors, nurses, teachers, aid workers, builders, seeing the difference that their love and their expertise are making, thanking God for the privilege of sharing what they have with others. I have in my office a photograph of smiling, excited children from our church presenting boxes of toys they had given for the 'Operation Christmas Child' appeal. All these people, of all ages, all situations, are reflecting a loving, caring God, powerfully and practically. God is right here on earth as well as in heaven, active in his world, sharing in the suffering, reaching out in healing, forgiveness, love and mercy.

Is that the answer? No, not totally, but it is part of it, that identification of God with us seen supremely in Jesus Christ. And we are in him, with him, through the Holy Spirit at work within us, and we always—yes, always—have the sure and certain hope of a joyful eternity, when all questions will be answered, all tears dried, all hurts healed, and all relationships restored. Where is God? At the centre, welcoming us home with love, enfolding us in his heart, his eternal purpose fulfilled. Until then we will never fully understand (nor should we) because what he asks of us is our faith and our co-operation. We can safely leave the rest to him, for there is no area of life, no activity that is untouched by that Calvary love, no darkness that cannot be dispelled by the light of life forever aflame by the power of the resurrection, the promise of his abiding presence.

For I am convinced that neither death, nor life, nor angels, nor rulers, nor things present, nor things to come, nor powers, nor height, nor depth, nor anything else in all creation, will be able to separate us from the love of God in Christ Jesus our Lord.
ROMANS 8:38–39

Father, life is so full of contradictions, it is sometimes hard to see any plan or purpose. In our confusion we dash here and there, searching for clues, for answers, for security; and when we fail we blame you, we doubt you, we get angry with you, we feel you are uncaring, unknowing and powerless to help. Then, gently but firmly, you put your arm around us and point us towards the cross, to Jesus, and we hear you say, 'Where am I? Here I am, have no fear, I will save you, trust me.' And in the looking and in the trusting we will find our peace and our joy.

Jesus said, 'Do not let your hearts be troubled. Believe in God, believe also in me... Peace I leave with you; my peace I give to you. I do not give to you as the world gives. Do not let your hearts be troubled, and do not let them be afraid.'
JOHN 14:1, 27

Chapter 22

JUST A SECOND

One of my favourite characters in *Alice's Adventures in Wonderland* is the White Rabbit who dashes along, worrying about being late, before popping down holes, and finishing up in unusual places. No wonder Alice raced after him without a thought about where she was going or how she would ever get back. For, as we read in the story, 'she had never seen a rabbit with either a waistcoat pocket, or a watch to take out of it'. Little wonder she was 'burning with curiosity'! In her place I would have felt exactly the same.

Following a white rabbit with a complex about time landed Alice in all sorts of difficulties; but then it is just a story, and not the sort of situations we are ever likely to experience! We do not meet white rabbits with watches crying, 'Oh dear, oh dear, I shall be too late' as we go about our daily lives; but maybe we do meet fellow human beings held captive by time, who are always trying to catch up with themselves in case something terrible happens to them. And before we know it we can be hurtling after them and falling into even bigger and deeper holes and more frightening situations than Lewis Carroll could ever have dreamed up for Alice.

Perhaps today, more than ever before, our generation is obsessed with time—dividing it up into ever smaller portions, yet trying to cram more and more into it; making up time, finding time, beating time, doing time (and maybe that last expression, coming from prison vocabulary, is not too far removed from our relationship with that elusive term 'time'). We serve it rather than the other way round.

Two newspaper advertisements I saw recently illustrated only too well our preoccupation with time. One offered a high precision radio alarm clock, the product of 'the very latest space age technology' with nothing left to chance. In its timekeeping it claimed accuracy 'to within one second in a million years'. I did not rush to order one. Somehow it did not sound as friendly as my bedside ticker. The description of this guardian of time had a rather ominous, though super-efficient, sound to it, and in a million years I think I will have long since risen from my bed, and have ceased to be interested in the passage of time!

The second advertisement offered me, if I could afford it, a very special Rolex watch. It was a 'Lady-Datejust', a most beautiful creation, advertised with a quote from opera singer Kiri Te Kanawa, 'Time I value above all things. It just gets more and more precious', followed by a comment from the makers: 'As we have often observed in Geneva, people who value their time value their timepiece.'

I have no doubt that both these timepieces will fulfil their promises, efficiently and beautifully; but what is this thing we call 'time'? Why are we so captivated by it? What is the purpose of it all? The Olympic Games held in Sydney in 2000 were judged to be the 'best ever'. Records came tumbling, and I was awestruck at the tiny fraction of time that divided gold-medallists from the also-rans. Often part of a tenth of a second made all the difference, and as one athlete who came second by such a fraction of time commented after her race, 'Sadly, no one ever remembers who came second, they only remember the winner.' Less than a heartbeat decides whether they shine for ever in the history of the Olympics or disappear into obscurity like a leaf in the wind. We may not be Olympic athletes, very few are, but we all seem to have this nightmarish concern about time. Why is it we are chained to it, rather than allowing ourselves to be free to enjoy it?

As I look back to the year 1999 I remember the quickening pace, every time I saw the word 'millennium'. It made me put a spurt on, and life began to have a desperate feel about it. It felt like the Christmas rush magnified a million times, almost as though if I had not done everything, completed every task I had set myself before 31 December 1999, I would fall into a big black hole from which there would be no escape. It was called 'millennium fever'; most people caught it, and it was highly contagious. Yet 31 December 1999 came and went, the year 2000 came and went, and we breathed again, and marvelled that we could! Now, perhaps, we can smile at our futile efforts and learn from our mistaken conviction that we had it within us either to halt or accelerate the march of time. We are beginning to realize that there is a better way of viewing and using time.

Pete is a big man in every way. An ex-policeman, member of our local village church, he is a man of few words, but what he has to say is always valuable, always touches the heart of the matter. He walks as he speaks, steadily, without rushing, a measured pace, born of his many years 'on the beat'; and now as he copes with his health problems he loves walking, looking, reflecting on what he sees and feels, and sharing it with others. The other day when I met him out on a walk he said, 'I'm trying to be a bit quieter, I think sometimes I'm too noisy. I need to be quiet and listen more, because when you're quiet and you listen then you can hear the birds singing, and you can hear other people too.' Pete is a man who hears birds singing and he hears other people too, and it shows in his life, in his steady, loving, dependable character. He knows what really matters. Time doesn't come into it. Instead it is that quality of living that matters, looking, listening and sharing.

Time given to listening, reflecting, seeing, understanding, needs to come first, before jumping into decision-making, action-taking, time-chasing—that life-sapping activity so often gets us nowhere, but drops us into another black hole of frustration and chaos. I find it is the Petes of this world who restore my sense of worth and balance as I too struggle with time. Thank God for those who hold up their hands against the mad rush of human traffic and in God's name and for our sake say, 'Stop!'; who redirect us away from the teeming motorways of life, to the quieter, more rewarding and ultimately safer routes, enabling us to enjoy our journey through each day in the company of our fellow travellers, and to arrive at our final destination in peace.

For thus said the Lord God, the Holy One of Israel:
In returning and rest you shall be saved;
in quietness and in trust shall be your strength.

ISAIAH 30:15

Lord, I know how important it is to pace myself, or rather, to allow you to be my pacemaker. But I need to get things done, I need to be in two places at once, I need to get ahead, I need to... I need to stop and think before dashing ever onwards, chasing after the elusive white rabbit called 'time' who doesn't really exist but who is the expression of my own fears, whose urgent tones are but echoes of my voiceless anxieties. Help me to see that time is a gift, to be enjoyed, to be savoured, to be shared. Help me to experience time as part of your eternity, knowing that there is, and will be, always enough, and more besides. It is not controlled by man's invention nor by human design, but by you, for your good pleasure, and for the living space of all creation. So here I am, Lord. Take my hand, and lead me at your pace, in your time to where you want me to be.

Make me to know your ways, O Lord;
teach me your paths.
Lead me in your truth, and teach me,
for you are the God of my salvation.

PSALM 25:4–5

Chapter 23

ALL ONE FAMILY

The Tenerife midday sun beat down fiercely, so I decided to seek some shady respite from the heat and glare. I wandered into the little Catholic church in the square, which was an oasis of quiet coolness, and sat down near the back, by the open door. A small group of people were gathered at the front of the church and the white-robed priest was talking to them quietly. Then I noticed the girl at the centre of the group, holding a very small baby in her arms. The girl was beautiful, her face aglow with serene happiness, and the young man beside her was gazing so proudly at her and the baby. My Spanish is non-existent, but I realized that I had walked into a baptism service. I wondered whether I should leave quietly, but as I made a move several of the group turned and smiled at me, and I took that as an invitation to stay. I had no problem following the service for the symbolism spoke for itself. The baby was anointed with oil, and the parents and godparents accompanied the priest to the font where the baby was duly baptized 'in the name of the Father, the Son and the Holy Spirit'. The father received a lighted candle, and the little family was given a special blessing, before they rejoined the rest of the group for the prayers and final blessing. Handshakes were exchanged all round and then off they went, no doubt to celebrate the great occasion.

Later that day I went to another service in the same church, this time for the most English of English services, Evening Prayer, led by the Anglican chaplain. The congregation comprised of visitors and 'ex pats', for Tenerife has a large community of British people, mainly retired, and we visitors were made to feel welcome and at home—just as I had felt welcome and at home that morning, too, language and denomination no barrier to being part of the Lord's family, sharing together in the Lord's house on the Lord's day. Each time I passed that little church during the week I thanked God for the brothers and sisters who worshipped there, and prayed for that child whose baptism I had witnessed, that she would grow to know and love the Lord and serve him faithfully throughout her life.

That Sunday brought back memories of many other places in the world where I have shared in praise and worship with fellow Christians, such as South Africa, Denmark, Italy, Austria, Germany, Madeira, Cyprus, and our Lord's own land, Israel. A wide variety, and yet always that same sense of belonging, learning, sharing and giving. During my life I have worshipped in so many different places, with people of all shades of expression, a rich kaleidoscope of the Christian family which for me is a foretaste of heaven. Hardly a week goes by when I am not involved in sharing with others outside my home church. In my work as York Diocesan Mothers' Union chaplain, I have the pleasure and privilege of meeting members in cities, towns and villages, in their worshipping communities. I have enjoyed sharing as a 'visiting preacher' from Shetland to Devon and all stations in between. I have lost count of the pulpits I have climbed into and out of, the vestries my robes have been unpacked and packed in, the hands I have shaken, and the cups of tea and coffee I have drunk afterwards. Memories of the prayers and music, the sounds and silences, and most important of all, the sharing in holy communion, strengthen my life, enabling me to keep on my pilgrim way in such joyful company, 'all one in Christ Jesus'. There is the joy, too, of welcoming others into our family church in Selby, and the village church where we live, to learn from them, to share their experiences of faith. Over and over again I hear them say, 'I have felt so at home here', to which I always reply, 'So you should, because you are.' It's not just a case of 'consider yourself at home', but of knowing the reality of it.

As one of the honorary chaplains at York Minster I meet people from every part of the world, and I always preface my prayers by saying, 'Whether you have come from across the road or across the world, you are part of God's family. I welcome you in his name.' Time and time again people come up and quietly say, 'Thank you for that, it meant so much to me.' As I celebrate holy communion in the Minster and look around at the people gathered for that midday service, I realize that it is a unique occasion. Never again, this side of heaven, will this particular group of people, unknown to each other, from all over the world, be together in this way. Strangers, and yet they are fellow pilgrims, sharing in that most intimate and holy sacrament of God's grace, through Jesus Christ, receiving those tokens of his love together, within the peace of the Lord. We have such a short time together, half an hour or so, and yet in that space, caught up into eternity, past, present and future, we are blessed by the peace of the Lord, and then sent out to 'go in peace, to love and serve the Lord' wherever our various paths take us. We are 'all part of life's rich tapestry', and what a rich tapestry it is that God gives us to contribute to and so to enrich the whole.

I feel a great sadness when I see some churches and congregations so stuck in their ways that they believe they have the only way of worshipping God—sometimes even that they are the only 'real' Christians, and feel no need of others. They see no point in sharing, and as for contemplating any possibility of change, well, that is a 'no-go' area. Yet life is all about change. All the time we are changing, evolving, growing, developing. If we are not, then we are like a stagnant pool, neither use nor ornament. In Christian terms, at best we are immature, at worst blatantly disobedient to our Lord's command. As we are reminded in the first letter of John, 'The commandment we have from him is this: those who love God must love their brothers and sisters also' (1 John 4:21). And how can we say we love them unless we open our arms in welcome, in recognition of our common identity; until we step forward and go through different doors prepared to receive, learn and be blessed in a new and challenging way?

We do not need to wait for a holiday, a special event, but can share any time at the church round the corner, the chapel up the road, the hall in town. Of course, some elements will be different, perhaps not the style we are used to, the hymns sung at a different tempo, the service book—or lack of it—hard to understand; but that is part of the wealth and variety of expression of worship, giving praise to our living

God, as we celebrate together 'one Church, one faith, one Lord', and go forward into the world together to tell and show the good news in the power of his Spirit.

There is one body and one Spirit, just as you were called to the one hope of your calling, one Lord, one faith, one baptism, one God and Father of all, who is above all, and through all, and in all.
EPHESIANS 4:4–6

Lord, so often when I talk about 'the Church' I mean a group of people in a particular building, following the same pattern week by week. People I know and love, and am comfortable with, and they with me. A cosy, predictable relationship. But I know that this is but a tiny corner of the whole picture, a speck in the three-dimensional mystery of your body, the company of your witnesses, past, present and to come. From all ages, of all ages, colours, languages, backgrounds and experiences, expressing their love to you in a multitude of ways, offering to you all that they have and are, echoing the songs of the angels, rejoicing in the hope of heaven, reaching out with the good news of your love. I pray that you will enlarge my vision, enlighten my understanding, and energize my heart and will in the fellowship of your faithful people, that together we may proclaim your glory in the world today, and to all eternity.

Now to him who by the power at work within us is able to accomplish abundantly far more than all we can ask or imagine, to him be glory in the church and in Christ Jesus, to all generations, for ever and ever. Amen.
EPHESIANS 3:20–21

Chapter 24

TREASURE
SEEKERS

The straggling queue moved slowly down the road, around the corner and into the leisure centre. A stranger passing through town might have imagined that some disaster had occurred, necessitating people to leave their homes, taking with them what they could carry, for everyone seemed to be carrying bundles and parcels, even balancing large objects on bicycles. Looking at their cheerful faces and hearing the excited chatter and laughter would soon have established that this was no disaster, but some sort of a celebration; but what was in all those parcels and packages? Obviously the contents were very precious, for they were all holding on to them with extreme care.

Had the stranger looked more closely at the leisure centre, the answer would have become clear. It was the day the 'Antiques Roadshow' TV programme came to our town of Selby, and here were those who had responded to the call to bring their treasures, to find out more about them through the services of the knowledgeable experts, and discover their value. After all, they could have been sitting on a fortune all these years; and so Grandma's teapot, that odd-looking chair and the picture that had been up in the attic for years had been brought out, dusted down, packed up and taken along to the show. For some it proved to be a very rewarding day, even to their appearing on television, with their pride and joy now revealed in its true glory. For others, it was interesting, but no more, and for some it was a real disappointment, for they had secretly harboured illusions of grandeur, fuelled by subtle hints over the years about the family heirloom, only to discover it was either a fake, or a mass produced item of little or no value.

I was not in the queue but later in the year I watched with great interest the programme of that day in Selby, mainly (I have to admit) to see if there was anyone I knew on the programme, and how the programme makers would portray our town. I do watch the programme regularly, because I find it fascinating to see people's reaction to the news they are given. Some try to hide their emotions, but the delight or the disappointment breaks through in most cases. I am so glad when they can genuinely say, 'It does not matter how much it is worth. I love it, and would never part with it.' I admired the lady on a recent pro-gramme who, on being told her piece of china was worth five thousand pounds, said, 'I am not sure what I shall do, but I would like a holiday!' I have sometimes felt I would like to put my arms round someone when they have been told they had a very valuable article, but had ruined it, and devalued it by their treatment. One poor soul who had so lovingly polished up a statue sat there holding her head in shame as she admitted she was the culprit. I wanted to say, 'Never mind, you did what you thought best. Does it matter?' I remember my mother being told many years ago that she had halved the value of a piece of furniture through constantly polishing it, and her reply was, 'I love that piece, I enjoy making it shine so beautifully. It is a labour of love, and so what if I have halved its value in money? It has given me a thousand times more pleasure just to polish it and enjoy it.'

I often feel sad when I see toys brought to the show in immaculate condition, still in their original boxes, which adds greatly to their value for collectors, but I wonder what the child felt when they were given a toy or doll they could not play with because it was too good! Teddy bears and dolls, train sets and model cars, 'as good as new', loved and admired from a distance, away from sticky fingers and dribbled kisses. I am proud to say my teddy was threadbare, and had to have frequent stitching up and restuffing, eyes sewed back, and clothes replaced because he was loved to bits, and gave me so much comfort and pleasure that he was beyond price. We all view things through our own eyes, in our own way, but how do you put a value on anything? Surely it is its intrinsic value, not in mere monetary terms.

There is nothing wrong with things, to enjoy their beauty, comfort, and charm. We can gaze at them, use them and share them, delight in all they represent, but at the end of the day they are dispensable props. A photograph in a newspaper recently showed the burnt-out remains of a lovely old country house, beside which a man was standing with his wife and two young children, the man's arms protectively around his family. The report described the fire tragedy in which the house and its contents, running into millions of pounds, had been destroyed, including unique paintings and documents, but the caption read, 'Thank God everything that really matters was saved—our lives.' That family had escaped in just the clothes they stood up in, but they were alive, and together; they had everything they needed, and they were thankful.

We live today in a possession-oriented society, where we are judged on what we have or own. Children 'must have' designer label clothes and footwear, otherwise they are not accepted by their peer group, and parents are almost blackmailed into providing these, even when they are well beyond their budget or the children's needs. We are constantly being wooed by seductive advertising which assures us that if we buy this, that or the other then we will be happy, highly regarded by others, in a position of power; and of course we do not need to pay for it until the year after next. So we amass these so-called highly desirable goods and we are surprised to discover that once the initial pleasure has subsided we are left with only the worry of the fast-approaching demand for payment. Television programmes pander to our acquisitive preoccupation. 'Who Wants to Be a Millionaire?' is compulsive viewing and the National Lottery is now a way of life for millions in our country.

This week I was sitting having a drink in our church coffee bar with a couple of elderly ladies, and one was telling us that her neighbour had been burgled, a common enough offence in the area. She said, 'In our day you could leave your front door open day and night and no one would lay a finger on anything. Folk were honest then.' Her friend gave her what I term 'an old-fashioned look' remarking sagely, 'It weren't

115

anything to do with honesty. It were common sense. None of us had owt worth pinching!' She had a point!

The people of Jesus' day had few material possessions, but what little they had was their insurance for when they fell on hard times, as there were no benefits to be had in those days. So a wedding dowry, pieces of jewellery, gold coins, or some fine material, if they had any, was very carefully stored and protected. The worry was always that it might be stolen, lost, eaten by insects, destroyed by time or conditions. These things were not status symbols, for mere ornamental purposes, but their owners' total security for the future, a major preoccupation. Jesus warned people of the danger of being so preoccupied with these things that they lost out on what really mattered in life. It was, as we say today, 'a matter of getting their priorities right'. Did they heed the warnings? Do we? Things can be very useful servants, but demanding masters, taking us over if we are not careful.

The people of Israel were provided with food in the wilderness, enough for each day, but when they tried to hoard it, it went bad, 'it bred worms and became foul'. They had to learn the lesson of trusting God for each day. We pray, 'Give us this day our daily bread', but we do like to have it in reserve for tomorrow, next week, next year. Our hearts are often packed tight in our deep freezers and store cupboards, in stocks and shares, bank accounts, in antique chairs and porcelain plates, or the treasure on four wheels in the garage. Our hearts and hopes are fixed on them, and they have become our gods, without our realizing it has happened. We have succumbed to the world's fatal attraction.

I am not suggesting that we get rid of all our possessions. I believe God has given us material gifts to enjoy, so long as we recognize them as disposable gifts and not permanent rights. These things have no currency value in the kingdom of heaven. If we will look beyond this life, with all its charms, then we will be able to enjoy the things of this earth, sitting light to them, setting our true ambition on realizing the kingdom of God.

Jesus said, 'Do not store up for yourselves treasures on earth, where moth and rust consume and where thieves break in and steal, but store up for yourselves treasures in heaven, where neither moth nor rust consumes and where thieves do not break in and steal. For where your treasure is, there your heart will be also.'
MATTHEW 6:19–21

Father, sometimes I act like a spoilt child. I grab what I want, I hoard things, I try to make myself seem important by what I possess. Yet without you I have nothing, I am nothing. I have no security, no future, apart from your love—and that you give in full measure, unreservedly, constantly. Lift my eyes, my thoughts, my desires away from the baubles of earth to the attaining of your kingdom, so that my heart may be set where true and lasting joys are to be found, through Jesus Christ, your Son and my Lord.

Whom have I in heaven but you?
And there is nothing on earth that I desire other than you.
My flesh and my heart may fail,
but God is the strength of my heart,
and my portion for ever.
PSALM 73:25–26

Chapter 25

FALLING LEAVES

If there is one time in the year when I feel gloomy, it is late autumn. I can almost put a date on it: the day we put the clocks back. Part of me rejoices in that extra hour in bed, but the rest of me shivers at the thought of ever-decreasing light, the problems of the approaching winter, and the panic feelings about Christmas shopping, and when I will have time to make the Christmas cakes as well as fit in everything else.

But it is more than this, it is a kind of melancholy, a feeling of loss and regret. I feel a failure because I have failed to fulfil my own expectations, the promises I had made to myself when the year was young, the sky was blue, and time seemed endless. Now, as I watch the autumn leaves drifting down, or being blown into a frenzy by the shrill wind, I see my intentions, plans and hopes falling with them, as much use as those leaves, fit only to be brushed up and discarded, or burnt on the bonfire. Life has a drabness and dullness, I feel as though I am plodding through porridge, physically, mentally and spiritually. I try to comfort myself by the thought, 'It is the time of year, I am not alone', and avidly read articles which describe these symptoms as related to the lack of light and sun, a bodily chemical reaction related to exterior conditions rather than interior problems.

Sharing this with a friend some years ago, he said, 'Ah, the dark night of the soul; read St John of the Cross', which I did, and still do from time to time. But while I do know times of spiritual dryness in my autumnal depression I have never felt abandoned by God. Yes, there are times when he seems far away, but a 'wayside pulpit' message I once saw on a church notice board jumps out of my memory bank and gives me a knowing nudge: 'When God seems far away, guess who has moved?' I take the point and get it sorted, finding, as the prodigal son did, that once he turned for home he found his father was waiting for him with wide open arms. And that is true for all of us, God's sons and daughters: he is always there for us, to forgive, restore and renew us. So I know within myself that although my mood is real, and I do have these experiences of inadequacies, failure, lost opportunities, they are perhaps necessary, reminding me I am not the paragon of virtue, fount of wisdom and spiritual 'know it all' that in my wilder flights of fancy I am sometimes tempted to imagine.

As I look out of our back window on to the school playing field I see the children rushing around in the watery autumn sunshine. Playing, chasing, shouting, their eyes bright with excitement, their energy unharnessed, imagination running riot. Crying as they fall over, but picking themselves up, or being picked up, for the tears to be wiped away, and then, muddied and scuffed, dashing back into the action, the sound of their laughter echoing across the field. Autumn has no feeling of sadness or regret for them; falling leaves are to have fun with, to be crunched through, thrown high into the air; cold puddles of water are to be splashed around, jumped in, not worrying about getting wet or dirty. Such things do not come into a child's reckoning, and why should they? Jesus reminded those who would know the secret of eternal life that they had to become like children, open, trusting, adventurous. The same message comes to us today as we pretend to be so sophisticated and self-sufficient—that we need to regain our real identity as a child of God. As a 19th-century hymn written by J.D. Burns puts it, 'That I may read with childlike eyes truths that are hidden from the wise.'

God has so many ways of getting through to us, and not always in the way we expect. It was a *Daily Telegraph* article on 'Britain's weather —what lies behind our autumn displays' by Philip Eden that gave me a new understanding, breaking through my gloom. He wrote:

Autumn used to be my least favourite season. Then one year while working in the Middle East, I returned to Britain for

119

some leave towards the end of October. The drive home from Heathrow was a revelation. The brilliant autumn colours set against a crystal clear blue sky, the early morning sunshine slanting brightly through the trees. Why had I never noticed this before? It was, perhaps, an illustration of the truism that you have to be deprived of something to appreciate it properly.

He went on to explain the changes and the delights of autumn, which hold within them the promise of new life. Now of course I knew that, in my head, but suddenly it all dropped into place. The leaves were symbols of new life, new opportunities. Like the autumn leaves, I needed to allow the old leaves, the past, to detach, fall, be blown away so that God could make known to me afresh his 'all things new'. I cannot say my dislike of autumn has gone completely. Those gloomy feelings do creep up on me at times, but I get the message! It was revealed not through some great volume of theology, examination of scientific data, or chronic introspection, but a newspaper article on 'the colour of home'.

Life is not wall-to-wall sunshine. It would be very dull if it was, with nothing to disturb or excite us. Each day would be a repeat of the one before, with the certainty that tomorrow and all the other tomorrows would be the same. It would be so easy then to let life drift by, without question. Thank God for highs and lows, the seasons of our lives, in which through his grace we can know the healing release of what is over and done, enabling us to rejoice in the new life springing up within us, the fresh experiences of his glorious purpose.

For everything there is a season, and a time for every matter under heaven… that which is, already has been; that which is to be, already is; and God seeks out what has gone by.
ECCLESIASTES 3:1, 15

Lord, thank you for the seasons of the year, each one holding its special gifts and joys, part of the natural cycle of creation and re-creation. They bring us reminders of our own cycle of life, from our birth, through the years of growing, learning, to maturity, and then letting go, returning to you, the source of our life, to be part of your new life for ever.

Teach us to welcome each new phase of our lives, to greet our autumn and winter as cheerfully and joyfully as we did spring and summer, knowing you are with us and in us, now, and for all eternity.

Then the angel showed me the river of the water of life, bright as crystal, flowing from the throne of God and of the Lamb through the middle of the street of the city. On either side of the river is the tree of life, with its twelve kinds of fruit, producing its fruit each month; and the leaves of the tree are for the healing of the nations.

REVELATION 22:1–2

Chapter 26

OUT OF THE
FLOOD

The ferocious storms and relentless torrential rain in November 2000 brought flooding to many parts of Great Britain. Day after day the country was pounded, every news bulletin showed yet more pictures of the devastation caused, and the reports were flashed around the world, so that as it was happening here people the other side of the world were viewing it too. Perhaps it is a cliché to talk about a global village, a small world, but through the highly developed global communications system, everything is immediate. Places unheard of before become household names, surely giving a sense of the importance of geography to everyone, unlike those dull and dusty books and globes we gained our information from when I was young.

Coverage of the floods in York, a mere fifteen miles from Selby, brought home to us how close they were getting. Scenes of the archbishop's palace at Bishopthorpe sitting in the middle of a giant lake, with the archbishop stacking sandbags, proved to us that no one was immune, and soon Selby was suffering the same fate. The army moved in, the electricity went off for varying stretches of time, many people were flooded out and evacuated, and life changed dramatically. Yet there was good humour and fun—'keeping your spirits up' as it was well described. The archbishop, Dr David Hope, wrote in the *York Diocesan News*:

Even in some of the worst hit areas there has been humour, which keeps the human spirit going in the very worst of circumstances. I noticed as I waded in the deep waters of

Malton/Norton a lifebelt on one front door, with the inscription 'Titanic—good luck!' And certainly the floods have brought out some of the best qualities of what we mean and understand by good-neighbourliness.

That was certainly evident during that extremely difficult and wearing time.

A memory that makes me smile comes from my not quite hearing what was being said to me. At our church we got away quite lightly from the floods, or so I thought when I was standing in what seemed a perfectly dry vestry. I remarked to Ann, one of our wardens, how pleased I was about that. 'Oh no,' she said, 'it's soaking under here, where all the water has come in.'

'How did it get in?' I queried.

'It's all the ducts,' she replied.

I had a vision of all those little ducks bobbing around under the vestry floor. 'Ducks, how did they get in there?'

She looked at me rather strangely and said, 'They've always been there.'

It seemed a very odd story to me. I had never seen any ducks around, and anyway, how could they survive under there, floods or no floods?

'So what sort are they?' I wanted to know.

Ann looked puzzled, obviously wondering what that had to do with it. 'The heating ducts under the floor—and the boiler house is flooded.'

How could anyone—apart from me, perhaps—confuse ducts with ducks? But you try saying those two words, and you will find there is only the very slightest difference in how they sound.

A fun story, but also a serious reminder of how easily we can totally get the 'wrong end of the stick'. Misunderstandings can happen through the mishearing of a word, reading the wrong body language, an imagined slight or rejection, and relationships can be destroyed, more damage caused than by a flood. Over and over again I meet sad and lonely people, embittered because of something that happened, or that they imagined happened, years ago; and now those feelings have hardened, almost shutting out any human possibility of reconciliation. If only it had been sorted out there and then, if one of them had had the grace to say, 'I am sorry if I hurt you, I didn't mean to. Let's forget it, and start again.'

In the Sermon on the Mount, Jesus urges us to sort things out quickly, making that a priority even before 'offering your gift at the altar'. That is how much importance Jesus places on our relationship one with another. Sometimes it takes a crisis or a tragedy to bring home the truth of that but how much better to live in a right relationship all the time, and enjoy each other, in love and harmony.

During the floods many people were brought together again, often through the media coverage and by friends and relatives getting in touch again, some after many years. One lady told me of the joy of receiving a phone call from cousins in Canada she had not heard from for many years, but they had been concerned for her, and located her again. 'We are not going to lose touch again,' she told me. 'In fact we hope to be able to meet again next year. That will be wonderful!' Another elderly gentleman was thrilled to hear from an old army pal, who in fact lived only a few miles away, and yet they had lost touch, but were now reunited. The way we respond to situations, especially difficult ones, can prove to be a real means of blessing, both for ourselves and for others.

In Psalm 84 we read:

> Happy are those whose strength is in you,
> in whose heart are the highways to Zion.
> As they go through the valley of Baca,
> they make it a place of springs;
> the early rain also covers it with pools.
> (Psalm 84:5–6)

We are all on our journey home, pilgrim people, making our way. We go through difficulties and hardships, through dusty valleys and floods of despair at times, but if we are centred on God, sensitive to his leading, obedient to his will, then even in those awful times we will be upheld, brought through, and even find cause to praise. There are springs in the dusty valleys, though often we have to dig deep to find them; but the result is of benefit not only to ourselves but to our fellow pilgrims. Then they can enjoy the spring water too, and come to praise the Lord for his provision.

God is our refuge and strength,
a very present help in trouble.
Therefore we will not fear, though the earth should change,
though the mountains shake in the heart of the sea,
though its waters roar and foam,
though the mountains tremble with its tumult...
The Lord of hosts is with us;
the God of Jacob is our refuge.
PSALM 46:1–3, 7

Lord, life is not always easy and predictable. Storms of all sorts can blow up without warning, in families, in communities, threatening to overwhelm and destroy. Yet so often in shared adversity we discover hidden reserves of strength, resilience, compassion. We see in each other examples of courage, love and faith. We are drawn together, renewed and energized for the future. In our failures and weaknesses we are reminded of our need for your wisdom and grace, and enabled to reach out and receive it. We rediscover the power of humour, the value of laughter to warm and cheer one another. Relationships are restored, new friendships bonded by facing challenges together, with and for one another. There are signs of your kingdom, glimmers of your glory, here with us, if we will but recognize them. And there are gifts to be shared, lessons to be learned, and memories that remain to sustain us in the days that lie ahead.

Now may our Lord Jesus Christ himself and God the Father, who loved us and through grace gave us eternal comfort and good hope, comfort your hearts and strengthen them in every good work and word.
2 THESSALONIANS 2:16–17

Chapter 27

SPOT THE
DIFFERENCES

Life gets very heavy at times, doesn't it?—or rather the reports of it that batter us through varying forms of communication. From the moment we open our eyes in the morning there is an endless torrent of news, views, information, warnings, appeals. No wonder we sometimes feel like crying out, 'Stop the world, I want to get off!' But then it doesn't, and we can't; but we can step sideways for a few minutes, to get a different viewpoint, and our breath back.

That is why I enjoy the puzzle pages in newspapers, generally to be found near the back, tucked away. A crossword or two, a quiz, some cartoon pictures, nothing too demanding or meaningful, just an aid to relaxation. I am not a *Times* or *Telegraph* crossword solver. They seem too much like hard work for me, although I admire those who not only solve them regularly, but with great speed. No, mine are the humbler, 'middle of the road' ones, and even those are only attempted when I am on a train journey, stuck in a waiting room or rather lacking in desire for intellectual activity. We all need such release, I tell myself. Undemanding, plain and cheerful moments of useless activity, and being able to achieve success through simple things. There is a degree of satisfaction in being able to fill in all the squares, a pride of completion, of a job well done, even though any youngster could have done it in half the time. I also happily tackle the 'spot the differences' pictures, which are skilfully drawn so as to make some differences very obvious, but others so tiny, so obtuse, that they prove quite elusive, teasing the eyes, challenging the ability to discern one picture from the other. 'Wasting time', you could call it, avoiding the serious demands of 'real life', escapism—but then why not?

When I find myself becoming over-serious and preoccupied with issues beyond me I take heart from some words of Rabbi Lionel Blue, many years ago, when observing that religious people of all faiths are inclined to take themselves far too seriously, and get very uptight in the process. He gave some shrewd and kindly advice: 'Practising your faith is like learning to ride a bicycle or dealing with your constipation. It's all right if you relax.' Remembering his words always makes me laugh, relax, and be thankful for the Rabbi Blues of this world who prick our pomposity so accurately and delightfully. So I make no apologies for admitting spending time on such relaxing trivia as spotting the differences. In fact, such an activity may well strengthen my powers of observation, which can provide awareness of the changes in my own life and of the world around me. Those small, seemingly insignificant changes can make the greatest difference for good or ill in the way I see and handle my life.

In Selby we have a learned and enthusiastic local historian. Through his articles, photographs, talks and slide shows, Richard keeps us all aware of our 'bygone days'—where we have come from and the changes over the years. Sometimes he uses twin projectors so that we can see places and situations as they were and as they are now, skilfully superimposing the present upon the past, often revealing changes we had not realized were happening. Some changes in our lives are so dramatic and life-changing we cannot fail but to recognize and be deeply affected by them; but for the most part change comes slowly, quietly, unnoticed.

The physical world around us is on the move all the time. It does not remain constant. There are the climatic changes which are exerting powerful influences upon our lifestyle; technological changes which influence work and leisure; changing attitudes to what have always been considered basic fundamentals of life; often a gradual erosion of beliefs, values and practices honed over the centuries. For example, Sunday and holy day observances; ethical issues which touch on the giving and the taking of life, such as implants, transplants, sperm banks, euthanasia. All these, and many other issues, have been viewed differently over the course of time, but the changes in attitudes have come so imperceptibly as to be unnoticed until they have completely altered the whole picture of life.

Life is different from how it was fifty years ago, ten years, last year; and in many cases we are glad it is so. The things I take for granted today, which have made my life fuller, safer, easier, were unknown in the early days of our married life, and when we were bringing up our children. They in turn delight in so many new aspects of the 21st century that I will never thoroughly come to terms with, although I do try. Spotting the differences gives me cause both to groan and to rejoice, but the main thing is that I recognize them for what they are, and evaluate them, rather than accept them without question.

I am part of the world as it is, and so are you, and whatever we may think, we are affected by it as children of this earth, this present generation, living out our citizenship within its parameters. But as we are reminded in the catechism, according to *The Book of Common Prayer* by baptism we are 'a member of Christ, the child of God and an inheritor of the kingdom of God'; and that is not subject to the fluctuations of the world, the Church or society. 'Learn to possess your possessions' was the challenge constantly thrown out to me as a young Christian by a saintly old minister. At the time I did not really understand what he was talking about, but those words ring ever more powerfully in my ears and heart as I continue along my pilgrimage in this 21st century, and my spiritual possessions become even more precious and worth defending and extending. I pray for God's help in what is described as 'all the changes and chances of this mortal life' in recognizing the place where I need to centre, to stand firm.

There is a difference we can make, whoever we are, by standing up for what is right, obeying God's word, and giving ourselves whole-heartedly and unreservedly to his service. As others look at those of us who dare to call ourselves Christians, can they see that our faith makes any difference? It is for us to make sure that they can, and that they do not have to look too hard or long to find it.

I appeal to you therefore, brothers and sisters, by the mercies of God, to present your bodies as a living sacrifice, holy and acceptable to God, which is your spiritual worship. Do not be conformed to this world, but be transformed by the renewing of your minds, so that you may discern what is the will of God—what is good and acceptable and perfect.
Romans 12:1–2

Lord, in the world of today it is often difficult to know which way to go, what to do. So many demanding and enticing voices insist that they have the answer to the world's ills, and that I need to adjust to their pattern, conform to their image if I really want to make a difference. 'A little more to the left here, a little more to the right there…'. But where are you? What have you to say?

You are where you have always been, right at the centre, and you call me to follow you. You have not changed, your message is still the same as it was two thousand years ago, and always will be, until the end of time. Help me to see what really matters and give me the strength to follow it, not in conforming to the world's ideas, but being transformed into your image, living your risen life, making a difference here and now through your power at work within me, to your praise and glory.

And when you turn to the right or when you turn to the left, your ears shall hear a word behind you, saying, 'This is the way, walk in it.'
Isaiah 30:21

Chapter 28

THE MISSING LINK

It had been a well-attended meeting, chaired confidently and efficiently, giving all the members the opportunity to make their points, or add their comments to the various items on the agenda. No hassle, no falling out, no disagreements, and no life! It started on time, finished on time, and in between we met—or did we? I wonder…

It reminded me of what the late David Watson said many years ago about the Church having a 'billiard ball mentality', individuals bouncing off one another merely to land in their own pocket. I was as guilty as anyone else, going along with the hidden agenda which was not to rock the boat, just keep it afloat and well-anchored, not getting anywhere or achieving anything apart from survival.

I fear much of our life is like that! Not just in churches but wherever groups, organizations, committees, councils and the like come together. Paperwork flies here and there, people rush hither and thither, clutching those pieces of paper, and the result? More pieces of paper, more files cluttering up the place, and the result is nothing. A sterile force, deadly dull, stultifying thought and action. What is the missing link, the something that would bring it all to life?

The answer was brought home to me when visiting a church some miles away. Arriving early, I did what I suppose we all do on these occasions—I scanned their notice board to get an idea of what was going on there. They had just embarked on a major project, which would not only be of enormous value to the church, but more importantly, to the whole community. It was not cheap, either in financial terms or in the time and effort that would be required, as well as coping with all the upheaval that such a scheme would involve. It would affect the life of every member, and it was going to take a long time to complete, but everything about it was so positive. They had obviously got a watertight plan of action!

Underneath a large question mark was written, 'How will we raise the money?' And the answer: 'By faith, by prayer, by enthusiasm.' Crisp, straightforward and to the point. It seems to me that those three words, 'faith', 'prayer' and 'enthusiasm' should be written on every agenda, personal and corporate, if we would ever move forward. We have all we need in position, but it has to come to life.

In his book *Discipleship*, published 20 years ago (Hodder & Stoughton, 1981), David Watson wrote:

> Cardinal Newman once said that the Church is like an equestrian statue: the front legs are lifted up ready to leap forward, every muscle of the back legs is standing out and throbbing with life. As you look at the statue you expect it to spring forward at any moment. Unfortunately, when you come back twenty years later, it has not moved a fraction of an inch. Yet look at the early Church twenty years after the outpouring of the Spirit; they had moved forward by astonishing leaps and bounds. There was one simple reason: the power of the Spirit was with them. (*p. 112*)

Twenty years on from now, what will have happened through us, and all those groups that we belong to? No doubt they are all very worthy, but what will have been achieved?

If we have faith, even if it is only of the proverbial 'mustard seed' variety, we can and will move forward. When that faith is surrounded by, and bathed in prayer we will be strengthened to overcome obstacles, and given wisdom and vision to fulfil the task, and the enthusiasm that will make it a joy, not a chore. Far too often it seems that the work and witness in which we are engaged is done through gritted teeth, out of a sense of duty and the fear of being seen as 'uncommitted' by others. Guilt-ridden conscripts do not move mountains or even molehills, but by faith and prayer and with enthusiasm anything can be achieved. We need faith in God, in the rightness of the task and in our fellow workers, drawing strength and support through prayer—but what about 'enthusiasm'? What is it? No doubt, like me, you have met the so-called enthusiasts who are like bulls in china shops, causing havoc; but that is the wrong use of the word, for according to the *Concise Oxford Dictionary*, 'enthusiasm' is derived from a word translated as 'possessed by a god', and so an 'enthusiast' is one filled with the Spirit of God.

When the Holy Spirit came upon the believers on the day of Pentecost they became new people, 'enthused' by the Holy Spirit to share the message of Jesus Christ, equipped and sustained by his power, receiving a God-given energy for the task entrusted to them. On the day of Pentecost the Holy Spirit was released into the world for all believers, not just a chosen few, for special occasions, but for all people, for all time. As we affirm in the holy communion service, 'The Lord is here, his Spirit is with us'—here, now, in us. William Barclay in his commentary on the Acts of the Apostles (The St Andrew Press, 1953) wrote, 'We receive the gift of the Holy Spirit and in that power we can win battles we never thought to win and resist things which by ourselves we would have been powerless to resist' (p. 29). We can be like the equestrian statue Cardinal Newman described, but brought to life, high-stepping off the plinth, demonstrating grace, power and agility, freed to be real. God's Holy Spirit within us frees us to be real, fired with enthusiasm for all that lies ahead. Mission statements, synods and seminars, even challenging words from church leaders, will not change statues into living beings filled with enthusiasm unless the Spirit is within and the Spirit is given free rein to accomplish the task.

Frank Sinatra once reprimanded his son Frank Jr for singing without enthusiasm, saying, 'Don't ever let me catch you singing like that again, without enthusiasm. You're nothing if you aren't excited by what you're doing.' Maybe God is saying that to us as he looks at the Church of today. After all, he has provided us with the music of life; he has put a song in our hearts, and surely that should make us excited, and sing for joy. And if we do, then maybe others will join in too.

All who believed were together and had all things in common; they would sell their possessions and goods, and distribute the proceeds to all, as any had need. Day by day, as they spent much time together in the temple, they broke bread at home and ate their food with glad and generous hearts, praising God and having the goodwill of all the people. And day by day the Lord added to their number those who were being saved.

ACTS 2:44–47

Lord, when your Spirit came upon your Church on the day of Pentecost, they became different people, filled with power, love and enthusiasm, no longer afraid but bold and adventurous. They spoke out with authority, reached out with compassion, shared their lives completely, and sang your praises unashamedly and joyfully. When your Spirit came life changed completely. Today we say, 'The Lord is here, his Spirit is with us' and go on struggling, discussing and debating, making sure we do not set our sights too high, or our objectives too broad. We prefer to keep within the narrow confines of our own experience, to protect ourselves from being 'overstretched'. We take shelter in meetings, making sure the agendas keep within limits, and that any action plan is delegated to a sub-committee meeting 'sometime in the future'. We face nothing too demanding, to save our ourselves from being judged failures. We escape attention, we merge into the world at large, and our small corner in particular.

How different from those early days when your Spirit came in great power! Then your people lived dangerously, sacrificially, triumphantly, and even though it cost them everything, they gave gladly and joyfully; and your Church grew, spreading out to the far corners of the earth. And now we ask fearfully, 'Where do we go from here?' Revive and renew us by your Spirit. Give us a fresh vision and confidence that we may take our place in the ranks of your Spirit-filled, Spirit-led Church of today, travelling with joy the road you have set before us, sharing the good news of your salvation with all people.

Now the Lord is the Spirit, and where the Spirit of the Lord is, there is freedom.

2 CORINTHIANS 3:17

Chapter 29

CALLED TO ACCOUNT

I was sitting comfortably in my armchair, in a lazy, hazy, nothing-in-particular mood, flicking through the paper, when a headline jumped out from the printed page, and forced me to concentrate. 'Your country needs you for the Census,' it read, and there was a photograph of the Lord Mayor of York, surrounded by several smart, smiling and very efficient-looking men and women holding a document with the words 'Count me in' emblazoned across the front. I read the paragraph avidly. It explained about Census 2001 and the need to recruit census-takers, 'a force bigger than the Royal Navy, to count people the length and breadth of the country—the biggest ever peace-time job in Britain'. A task force to make sure we are all duly counted, and accounted for, not just as names and numbers but as to our situation, our opinions, how we are as people. On the basis of all this information essential services can be planned, strategies put into operation, and targets established, until the next time round, until the next great census takes place.

I did not feel moved to offer my services, even at a fee, as a census-taker, but I did feel admiration and sympathy for those who responded. It would be no easy task, all that foot-slogging and ear-bending, demanding very resilient and hardy individuals. So now we are all logged, graded, fed into the computers, and birthed as statistical information, so that our progress can be monitored and programmed. All very exciting, but what is new—apart from the technology? From the beginning of time the powers that be have seen fit to have everyone accounted for, neatly and safely bundled, to avoid anything, or anyone, getting out of hand and causing nasty or unexpected surprises. The Romans, of course, had got it to a fine art, as they did with most things. The Christmas story is all to do with a census-taking, and the Romans' attention to detail provided us with deep insight into the life and times of Jesus Christ.

The main difference between the census in or around 8BC and the one in AD2001 is that now the census-taker comes to our door. Back then, you would have been commanded to return to the place you originated from, which caused considerable hardship to many, including the elderly and infirm and, as in Mary's case, the pregnant. The Roman Empire was scattered and fluid, so the censuses, taken every fourteen years, enabled them to keep a check on the population, and were certainly valuable for the purpose of apportioning taxation. How else could the Roman system be upheld and sustained? As with us today, the money had to come from somewhere, and from someone.

Mary and Joseph had to make the journey from Nazareth to Bethlehem, which was about eighty miles. Not far, in today's terms, perhaps a couple of hours by road, even less by train—on a good day. There and back in the same day with time to spare for the traveller in 2001, but a long and arduous journey for the travellers two thousand years ago, by foot, donkey or mule, through difficult territory with the danger of robbers, wild animals, lack of food or water, and the problems of the climate. For Mary, almost at the end of her pregnancy, it would have been a desperately uncomfortable journey, a frightening situation, especially to be met with nowhere but an outhouse to deliver her baby. It was a strange beginning for her child, the Son of God, Lord of heaven and earth. There was no room for his birth, 'no place to lay his head' through much of his life either, and a borrowed tomb in his death. The prophecy in Isaiah 53 charts the life of the 'suffering servant' as clearly as any census of today charts our lives. Yet his story is still being recorded, his life still lived out through the power of the Holy Spirit here in our lives and times. Not on census forms, but in the lives of his people, and recorded in 'the Lamb's book of life', to be opened at the last day.

What is recorded in the census will provide essential information about your life and mine for official purposes. Assessments will be made about us, who we are, what we are; but all that information, however carefully noted, will not reveal the real us, our soul, our very being. When Jesus was here on earth he saw each person as they were. He knew the deep longings and desires of their hearts, he knew their failings and fears, and their sins. He saw through the hypocrisy—the 'acting out a part' as the dictionary defines it. He did not conduct a census or write anything down, but reached out and touched people, opening them up to self-knowledge in the light of God's truth.

He continues to do so today. He comes knocking on our door, the door of our life, standing before us, offering to enable us to begin a new chapter and wipe out all that has dragged us down and spoiled our lives. He stamps 'Account Paid' across the record of our misdeeds, because by his death on the cross he has redeemed us—paid the debt —and we can go free, saved from sin and its consequences.

When John was in exile on the island of Patmos he had an amazing and awesome vision of what was to come. It was a vision not just for him to see and hear, to learn from and to be encouraged, but to share, for the word that came to him was 'Write in a book what you see.' And we have that Revelation to John as the last book of the Bible, the last word to us of God's glory, of judgment, of grace, of power and life. Many find it a frightening book and shy away from reading or studying it. Scholars disagree about it, and it is full of imagery which is beyond our experience, but it far outweighs the difficulties when we read it prayerfully, with our ears and hearts attuned to what the Spirit is saying to us through it. The last two verses of the book, indeed of the Bible, are words of encouragement and hope to all those who would trust in Christ and follow him: 'The one who testifies to these things says, "Surely, I am coming soon." Amen. Come, Lord Jesus! The grace of the Lord Jesus be with all the saints. Amen' (Revelation 22:20–21).

Amen to that!

I am coming soon; hold fast to what you have, so that no one may seize your crown. If you conquer, I will make you a pillar in the temple of my God; you will never go out of it. I will write on you the name of my God, and the name of the city of my God, the new Jerusalem that comes down from my God out of heaven, and my own new name.

REVELATION 3:11–12

Lord, bulky brown envelopes fall through the letter box, demanding my immediate attention and return, sometimes with the added threat of a penalty if I fail to respond in time. Others are more pleasant, offering me free gifts, discounts, even the chance of a wonderful holiday if only I will fill in the forms, so as to enable them to serve me better—or so they assure me. 'Tell us everything—or else we will punish you severely.' 'Tell us everything, then we will reward you.' Threats and promises, wanting me to bare my soul, and my bank account, my likes and dislikes, the places I frequent, the brands I buy.

You do not send brown envelopes, but you come to me, in person, offering me all that I need to be the person I should be. There are no forms to fill in, no money to pay. All I must do is say, 'Come in. I need you, I want you, I welcome you.' You open your book, and show me what is written in it: my name, in your book, your book of life, inscribed with love. Thank you, Lord, for loving me.

'Rejoice that your names are written in heaven.'
LUKE 10:20

Chapter 30

JUST TEN
MINUTES

It is amazing, verging on the miraculous, what can be crammed into ten minutes of time. Ask any working mother as she juggles those precious minutes with the breakfast dishes still to be put away, the pile of dirty clothes to be put in the washer, the dog fed and watered, children to be organized into their school clothes, and their bags and kit found, before grabbing her bag and keys, combing her hair and putting on her lipstick. The businessman drives down the motorway arranging his diary, giving instructions and working out the terms of a contract by mobile phone, ten minutes in which to cram an hour of work, before opening his office door.

Those are only two instances of the 'do it in ten minutes' brigade, but it affects us all. Whatever our age or personal circumstances, we tend to cram into a few minutes far more than we should, most of the time engaged in several activities at once, without the eyes in the back of our head, the two pairs of hands and the superior mental power we wish we possessed. No wonder we get stressed, pulled in so many directions at once. We get frayed, not just at the ends, but in the middle as well, sometimes snapping under the strain. Yet each day is conveniently divided into 24 hours, allowing for work, rest and play, as a well-known confectionery producer once reminded us, extolling the virtue of eating their bars to enable us to make the most of our working, resting and playing hours. We subdivide those times, often with the work allocation grabbing a large portion from the other two. 'All work and no play' makes Jack and Jill not only dull people, but dangerous too; both to themselves and others, and although we may, and probably do, think we are the exception to the rule, we are not! I speak with the voice of one who still has not learnt the lesson either of her own words or experiences. All I can plead is, 'I am working on it.' But then perhaps that is the trouble. I am 'working on it', rather than stepping back, resting from it, and getting an overview, an extended field of vision.

Twenty-four hours in a day—and that means there are 144 ten-minute periods, which makes life quite manageable, for it does not have to be pressed into one or a few of those periods, but spread over the day, paced, spaced and enjoyed!

God has given me many blessings throughout my life, and one of them is the ability to sleep anywhere, at any time. In my days of travelling by train from Manchester to Macclesfield each day, I could 'drop off' at Bramhall and wake up in the tunnel approaching Maccles-field station—ten minutes of sleep which refreshed me for the rest of my journey home, either by bicycle or bus. That ability has never left me; I only have to say to myself, 'I'll just have my ten minutes' and I am asleep. As I have got older I sometimes have more than one period of ten minutes; and why not? I can recommend it. It has only struck me recently, the significance of that expression 'my ten minutes'. What about the other 143 periods of ten minutes each day? They are mine too, the gift of God, a day at a time. For sharing and service, yes—but when God gives us gifts, he wants us to use and enjoy them for ourselves as well. Why do we feel guilty about enjoying ourselves, taking time out, even for what we may term 'wasting time'? Surely these times give an elasticity to our lives, to enable us to take on board the demands and strains of each day, which we are all subject to. Ask anyone concerned with personal fitness about that, and they will tell you that expansion and relaxation are all part of the same process of building strength and maintaining it. Surely what is true for the body is true for the mind and spirit also.

When we read the Gospels, and study the life of Jesus, we see how incredibly busy he was, how demanding was his ministry. He had the constant pressure of people upon him and, knowing how short his time would be, the urgency of preparing his disciples to carry on his work; the need to spend time with them, teaching them, listening to them, sorting them out. Yet he enjoyed life, the company of friends, visiting, parties, sitting over a meal. In fact he was accused of being 'a glutton and a drunkard, a friend of tax-collectors and sinners'. He also made time to be alone, to get away by himself, to rest, to reflect. He was able to sleep even in a small boat in the middle of a storm. He knew the value of rest, the renewing power of sleep. Above all, he knew that first and foremost he needed, and wanted, to have time alone with his Father, to be with him, to listen, to enjoy their relationship. Even in the most difficult and demanding of times he got away to spend that time alone with God. Jesus was a whole person, and he sets before us the pattern of living that is as relevant for us in the 21st century as for him in the first. The way he set before us is the way of abundant living in every sense of the word.

In the Church of today, I fear we are far too busy doing so many things that we are apt to lose sight of what being the Church, 'the body of Christ', really means; of what the gospel is about, and of how we are meant to be sharing it. Instead we face mountains of paperwork, millions of man- and woman-hours of committees, councils, synods, planning and prattling. No wonder we get discouraged and disaffected and, in the process, ineffective too. We claim that in Christ we have 'a new life, a new lifestyle'—so where is the evidence? What can we offer to those outside, looking in? Does that new life give any answers, or just pose more questions?

Towards the end of 2000 the Archbishop of York called the diocese of York to share in his initiative entitled 'Living the gospel'. No doubt there were groans from those who thought they had heard it all before, and had had enough of initiatives. But from the beginning the initiative has fired and excited this part of the country, and I hope that the vision will spread to many other areas and churches. What set it alight for me, and I am sure for very many others, was that first and foremost the archbishop called on us to commit ourselves to the 'ten minute pledge' which he put like this: 'Doing our best to find ten minutes on most days when we will withdraw from the business of our day-to-day lives, and consciously put ourselves into the presence of God.'

Ten minutes for God. Ten minutes with God. Giving him our total, undivided attention, resting in his presence, relaxing in his love, and so being renewed for service. 'Ten minutes? Every Christian does that!' you may say, but I am not convinced that every Christian does. I know there are days when this one doesn't! Oh yes, I pray when I am driving, I think about God when I am preparing the lunch, I ask for guidance while I am in a difficult meeting, I praise him when I get out of a trouble spot. But that is not giving him undivided attention, it is squeezing him into time we are giving to other concerns, squeezing him out of the time that belongs to him. Time centred on God alone, before him in a quiet place, is giving him and ourselves time to be in fellowship and harmony, and for his will to be done in us. If we will give God just ten minutes a day out of the time he has given us, who knows what the effect might be on us, on the Church, on the world. There is only one way to find out, isn't there?

The apostles gathered around Jesus and told him all that they had done and taught. He said to them, 'Come away to a deserted place all by yourselves and rest a while.' For many were coming and going, and they had no leisure even to eat. And they went away in the boat to a deserted place by themselves.
MARK 6:30–32

And the Lord said, 'Come away…'. Lord, that is an invitation too good to be refused—or so we say, but then we are busy people, responsible parents and carers, engaged in our businesses, working in the community, supporting good causes, and being active in the Church. Life here in the 21st century is very different from when you issued that invitation to your disciples while you were here on earth. Times have changed, Lord—but then, of course, you know that, for you are the Lord of time. You know what we need to do with it and in it and that is why you remind us now of your invitation—of your command.

It wasn't always easy then, and it isn't always easy now. We cannot easily take time out. Not all of us can get into a boat, go up a mountain, or even leave the desk or kitchen sink. But for ten minutes, it is possible to step aside, to shut out the distraction of life, to find space. The time is there, you are there. What am I waiting for?

'Come,' my heart says, 'seek his face!'
Your face, Lord, do I seek.

PSALM 27:8

Chapter 31

ALL CHANGE

No one could remember a time like it. Even the very old people who had lived in the village all their lives, like their parents and grandparents before them, shook their heads, and said, 'It's never ever been like this.' What had been a gentle meandering stream through the village was now a raging torrent, rushing along like a wild monster, tearing away with powerful jaws at the grassy river banks, taking chunks out of it and spitting it back into the water. Pushing onwards and outwards, changing the quiet landscape into a muddy battlefield. The villagers did what they could, aided by those who had come to help them. Sandbags were placed along the banks, and beside the houses along the path. Furniture was moved upstairs, and animals rounded up and taken to higher ground. During those days there was little else anyone could do but take shelter, watch and wait.

Eventually the waters began to subside, the mopping up started, meetings were organized to decide future plans, and life gradually went back to normal—or as near to normal as was possible. Life would never be the same again, though. The gentle stream was now viewed through the eyes of experience, for what had been thought of as impossible had been proved to be a terrible reality. 'It could never flood here' was now 'When the floods came'.

It was still their stream, of course, loved for its place in the village, for all the pleasure it gave—the walks along the banks, the habitat for wild life, the playground for children, a view often recorded by artists and photographers. In summer when it slowed to a trickle it was hard to remember it in flood, but on stormy days, or through the weeks of steady rain in autumn and winter it was watched very carefully indeed, and the flood precautions were inspected regularly, those new protective measures that had been put in place after the floods. No, the stream could never be taken for granted now, nor its warning signs ignored. Perhaps in a strange sort of way it had gained a new dignity and respect, always being taken into account when plans and suggestions were mooted in the village. Lessons were learned from what had happened, horizons broadened, relationships strengthened through the sharing of those difficult days together.

The stream flows on, its water coming from high up in the Dales, flowing freely until further on it meets up with other streams and rivers and together they flow to the sea. It is a natural journey, but always containing within it an element of surprise; and for those along its route there is always the demand to 'take note', to live with it, to change and be changed by it. Water has a life of its own, ever changing, ever flowing onward to fulfil its purpose, always active, moving along, productive and at times destructive; but without it there would be no life, no future. Nothing can survive without water, and so we have to co-operate with it, use it wisely and imaginatively, respect it, and 'go with the flow'.

Water and time have much in common, flowing on, so often taken for granted, but then suddenly forcing us to realize their movement, their power. It is for us to adjust to them, not them to us. No wonder Isaac Watts reminded us that 'time, like an ever-rolling stream, bears all its sons away'—that same stream of time that we are part of here and now, and that we resist at our peril.

We embark on that stream of time from our conception, and we flow on through life both in the gentle passage of time and in its flood spate. We need to recognize that time is passing, life is changing, and to go forward, not resisting what is happening, but being imaginative, open, using it to the full and looking ahead, being prepared. An article I read some time ago by Baptist minister Steve Chalke was headed, 'Change is here to stay. Embrace the future or get throttled by it'. He says, 'Change is sweeping every aspect of life, not only in the UK but right around the world', and goes on, 'Change really is the only thing that is here to stay. But the sheer speed of change is new and presents the

144

Church with its biggest challenge' (*Woman Alive*). We have only to look at the explosion in the communications industries; and not only the machinery of it, the 'chips with everything' world, but the content and concepts. We see different thought processes, different mind activities, different responses. We may hark back to 'the old days', long to halt the tide of the third millennium, but we cannot; and if we try to do so we will be caught up, thrown out, and declared obsolete.

As Christians, of course, we rejoice in the security of 'Jesus Christ, the same, yesterday, today and for ever', but we have to move and grow and live in the freedom that this knowledge affords. The body of Christ is a living body; it moves, changes, develops, sustained by the living word of God, empowered by the living Holy Spirit within us. The heart of Christ beats within us, to fulfil his purpose here and now, leading, driving us onward, not always comfortable or safe in the short term, but showing the way to life as he intends for us.

Recently, at a meeting where we were having to face up to major changes in a particular situation, we were reminded that 'we have a God of all comfort, but not a comfortable God'. Those words come to me again and again as I struggle with changes in my own life, in my own personal situation as well as being part of the Church and various communities. Yes, of course, changes have always happened, and are happening as you read these words; but the difference between today and even ten, twenty, fifty years ago is that the changes occur more rapidly. Nothing is permanent, whether the climate, relationships, employment, leisure, means of transport, modes of thought and expression, the environment, people's attitudes. The meandering stream has become a torrent, and we are part of it. It's no use burying our heads in the sand, or our talents in the ground, out of fear of what might happen, or what others might say or think. At the end of the day we give an account of our life and times to God who knows, who understands our strengths and weaknesses, and has placed us here at a particular time and place to fulfil our full potential; and who has provided all we need to do so. God has given us all the equipment we need and the strength and ability to use it—all we need to 'go for it' with him, wherever he takes us. It is an adventure, and a joy, so long as we are unafraid of the flood or changing circumstances, if we are willing to be changed by him to meet the challenges of a changing world.

As Cardinal Newman wrote, 'Here below to live is to change, and to be perfect is to have changed often.' So let us live life to the full, and attain a perfect end.

The floods have lifted up, O Lord,
the floods have lifted up their voice;
the floods lift up their roaring.
More majestic than the thunders of mighty waters,
more majestic than the waves of the sea,
majestic on high is the Lord.

PSALM 93:3–4

Father, I like life to trickle on gently, with no hurry, no rush, just a pleasant stroll along the way. I can cope with that, enjoy its charms, in the company of like-minded people. But times have changed; the flow has increased, life thunders along like a torrent, taking me with it, and I am afraid, longing for 'the old days' and the old ways, safe and secure. I like life like that, the Church like that, the world like that; and I know it cannot be, for life means change. It has a purpose, a destination, and to be part of that I must learn to change, adapt, and ride with it and in it. The sounds and sights may at times terrify me, their power threaten me, but I hear and see you in your majesty and glory; you urge me on, you carry me forward, and I find I am not alone, but part of a great multitude, streaming onward, encouraging and supporting each other, drawing others into the adventure of faith and service, in the name of Jesus, and in the power of the Holy Spirit, now and for ever. Amen.

I will sing to the Lord as long as I live;
I will sing praises to my God while I have being.

PSALM 104:33

Chapter 32

BEGINNING
AGAIN

Nicodemus was a scholar, a Pharisee, respected for his wisdom and authority; a deep thinker, who did not accept ready-made ideas but reasoned things through for himself. Today, no doubt, he would have been a tutor at one of the Oxford or Cambridge colleges, or at least held a visiting professorship. He had an open and enquiring mind, and so he did not intend to pass judgment on Jesus until he had met him for himself, and discovered the source of his teachings. So a late-night private meeting was held between them. This is often thought to be because Nicodemus was afraid of what his fellow Pharisees would think of him for meeting with Jesus and talking with him openly; but it could simply have been so that they might talk together, in the cool of the evening, away from the demands of the crowds, the pushing and shoving in the heat of the day. I tend towards that view; but for whatever reason, they met alone and at night.

Nicodemus acknowledges that Jesus is a teacher, and one sent from God, for what he has done has shown that; but why, and how? Jesus tells him to understand that he must be born again. Nicodemus cannot grasp that. It does not make sense, it defies reason, and his incredulous response is, 'Can one enter a second time into the mother's womb and be born?' Of course not! But then what did it mean, and how could someone at the height of his powers and years go back to the beginning again? It was as impossible as the notion of a physical rebirth.

The story is told in a well-known biblical passage, of course, which repays frequent study, for it has been the means of many coming to understand the new birth, and experience it for themselves. Perhaps one of the best-loved verses in scripture is John 3:16: 'For God so loved the world that he gave his only Son, so that everyone who believes in him may not perish but may have eternal life.' That all-embracing 'everyone' includes all ages, all backgrounds, all time. So let me introduce Harry to you.

When I first met Harry, he was in his early seventies, a bluff, no-nonsense man. He had worked hard all his life, in fact his work had been his life, and now, sadly widowed, he had decided he needed a housekeeper. So Josephine, a widow, had taken him on, and one of the first questions she had asked him was 'Which church do you go to?'— which rather put him out, as he didn't. But, determined to do all he could to keep her, he used to drive her to church, drop her off, then pick her up afterwards; until one day he reasoned he would save time and petrol if he attended with her, and so he became a regular member of our congregation. Gradually I noticed how much he had changed. He was more at ease, entering into the life of the church, full of fun, always ready to help. I could see him growing in faith, wanting to know more, eager to learn; and later on, he and Josephine were married—a great day!

Then came the time when they decided to move to be nearer Josephine's family, and Harry was sharing with me how he had come to faith and that he intended to join the church where they were going. He said, 'It has meant so much to me being here, it has changed my life. I shall always be grateful; but do you know what I would have loved to have done? Read a lesson in church.'

I quickly assured him it was no problem, he could do so on his last Sunday.

He was thrilled, but said, 'I'll need a bit of help, some practice.'

'No problem, come down to the church and I'll take you through it.'

So, on a quiet morning that week, we had our practice, and very well he did too. Then we sat together in church and he said very quietly, 'I'm going to tell you something now I've never ever told another soul, not even my wife. Some time ago you preached on healing, and said you didn't need to be a deaconess or a vicar to lay hands on someone

148

and pray for them; anyone could do it, and pray to the Lord. I had a friend who was dying, in a lot of pain, and I used to sit with him while his wife went shopping. This day I was sitting with him and he was really bad, and I thought, 'I wish I could do something to help him', and I remembered what you had said. So I put my hands on his head and prayed, 'Please take away his pain, give him peace, in the name of Jesus.' After I had got home his wife rang and asked me how I had found him. I said he had been in a lot of pain, and she told me he seemed a lot better since I had been, in fact the pain had gone.' Harry looked at me, then said, 'And do you know, Mrs Cundiff? He never had any pain again. He died a couple of months later, but no pain, and quite at peace. I've never told a soul, because people would have said, "Silly old feller, what difference did that make?"—but it was an answer to my prayer, and it worked. You were right in what you said.'

I have respected Harry's desire for privacy, and when I have used the story of that healing I have changed his name, so no one knew it was him; but Harry and I often spoke about it and what it meant to both of us. Harry continued to grow in his faith, in the joy of the Lord, and became an active member of the church where they went to live. When again he was widowed he went to be with his wife's family, entering wholeheartedly into the life of the local church. He would ring me up and tell me what was happening, and was thrilled to be a regular lesson reader, a member of a Bible study group called 'The Church Mouse Lunch Club', and always took part in the nativity play each Christmas as the oldest shepherd. He had been 'born again' and delighted in his new life. The week before he died at the ripe old age of 98 he rang me, telling me how well the church was doing, what a grand vicar they had, and what a lovely lot of young people. 'I'm not so good, I can't get out now, but the vicar came and brought me communion on Friday,' he said, and then, 'God bless! Love to all.'

I think I knew then it would be the last time we spoke here on earth, and just days later his son rang to tell me he had died. The funeral, 'A celebration of the life', was held in his church. He had planned it all himself, and asked for 'no mourning, only celebration, and that there be no flowers, only donations', as this would be more beneficial. His four favourite hymns were sung: 'The Lord's my shepherd', 'Great is your faithfulness', 'Just as I am' and, to end, 'Come, ye thankful people come'. As his son said, 'It was an amazing funeral, a real celebration, lots of fun, lots of stories, and he had planned it all.' He had also planned that he would be brought back to Selby to be buried with his first wife, and that I would take the service, and so I did. Just a few of us stood on a lovely crisp sunny day and said our final goodbyes and thanks. As I stood there and remembered Harry I thought too of Nicodemus and his question, 'How can anyone be born after having grown old?' 'You ask Harry, he will tell you' was my answer—but then I am sure Nicodemus has made the discovery for himself.

Harry had already had his 'three score years and ten' when he made his great discovery and entered into that new birth. God gave him nearly thirty more years to enjoy it, to grow and become mature in faith, and to be such an encouragement to others, not least to me. The prayer of faith for his friend, that answered prayer, was not only a blessing to them but a means of strengthening my faith in the ministry of healing, in all its dimensions, even all these years later; and I am sure it always will be. Harry believed and acted. Thank God for him, and for all who take that leap of faith. Like a pebble in a pond, the ripples still flow out.

Now there was a Pharisee named Nicodemus, a leader of the Jews. He came to Jesus by night and said to him, 'Rabbi, we know that you are a teacher who has come from God; for no one can do these signs that you do apart from the presence of God.' Jesus answered him, 'Very truly I tell you, no one can see the kingdom of God without being born from above.' Nicodemus said to him, 'How can anyone be born after having grown old? Can one enter a second time into the mother's womb and be born?' Jesus answered, 'Very truly, I tell you, no one can enter the kingdom of God without being born of water and Spirit. What is born of the flesh is flesh, what is born of the Spirit is spirit. Do not be astonished that I said to you "You must be born

from above." The wind blows where it chooses, and you hear the sound of it, but you do not know where it comes from or where it goes. So it is with everyone who is born of the Spirit.'
JOHN 3:1–8

Lord, thank you that there is no age limit to being born again. No qualifications are required to enter your service, only the willingness to take you at your word, and to trust you in and for all things. Thank you for the gift of new life, the power of prayer and the joy of knowing and serving you, and for all the evidence of your grace that we see in the lives of others. May you reflect in our lives what you have given us and shown us, to your praise and glory, today and always.

'The promise is for you, for your children, and for all who are far away, everyone whom the Lord our God calls to him.'
ACTS 2:39

Chapter 33

HEAVENS ABOVE

It was a bitterly cold January night, the sort of night when you are glad to get indoors, pull the curtains, and turn up the heating. So what were all those people doing standing outside, gazing up into the sky? They all appeared very excited and animated, seemingly quite oblivious of the night chill.

I was attending a meeting of 'Churches Together', but just before eight o'clock the chairman declared a break so that those who wanted to could leave the meeting and stand on the pavement outside the hall, which most of us did; for we had more on our minds than the agenda that evening, something much more exhilarating. It was the first lunar eclipse of the 21st century, and the conditions, especially in the north of England, were perfect, with a bright clear sky, so that the wonder of the eclipse could be fully seen and enjoyed. Late evening, and the full moon began to dim as it entered the outer part of the earth's shadow. Gradually the darkest part of the shadow began to slip over the moon's surface, until finally it was completely covered. The moon took on a reddish hue, and not only that, a wonderful array of stars shone clearly; the north star, and the planets Jupiter, Saturn and Venus, and all the heavens put on a glorious display, while here on earth we wondered, marvelled, and delighted in it all. The cold was forgotten, the concerns of the day fell away, worries were put on hold, and for a few short hours the heavens and the earth were in glorious harmony, united in the wonder of all creation. Young and old alike were caught up in the thrill of it all, the beauty, the 'other-worldliness'.

I thought back to the summer of 1999 and the eclipse of the sun, which had been anticipated with such trepidation as well as excitement.

Dire warnings were issued about the dangers of looking into the sun, and special measures set up to combat any trouble, while very real fear was felt by many that this might be an omen, an ominous prelude to something beyond our control. I watched it while on holi-day in Italy, and there was a palpable feeling of tension that day. As it began to happen everyone stopped, sat down, huddled together, and you could almost hear hearts beating. Then as the darkness fell there was just silence, until as the light began to filter through again a great cheer arose from the crowd, a cheer of relief that it had happened, and we had come through it. How strange that the sun in summer being eclipsed had been frightening, the moon in winter exciting. But then the majesty of the sun, the moon and the stars affects us in different ways; and when we begin to explore what is happening we realize just how small and insignificant we are compared with what is beyond our own domain, our own little world.

Imagine what it must have been like in centuries gone by, when the elements were always seen as omens of the gods, light expressing pleasure, and darkness dire warning of doom and destruction. An. eclipse would be terrifying, unlike today when we have a surfeit of information, the dates and times pinpointed by those who have made it their life study; when human beings have pushed out the bounds of exploration and discovery, combined with all the modern scientific equipment that enables them to go where no one else has gone, to see what no one else has ever seen, and to come back and tell us. Yet in spite of all this we realize that we have but scratched the surface of knowledge and understanding. We, as human beings here on earth, are minute particles, less than grains of sand on the shore, fragments of earth. We imagine we are so big, so important, so powerful, as we scurry around; but when we look into the sky we are cut down to size, or rather, we realize what we are in relation to infinity.

However we may try to define the building blocks of life and their purpose, we have to come back to creation, and to accept that they were brought into being by a power so great as to be beyond our under-standing. That power was and is God, both all-powerful and yet one who can be known even by us, here and now. In the book of Genesis the account of creation is simple enough for a child to understand and mysterious enough for the wisest to stand in awe and amazement, showing that all things are but part of God's creation, speaking to us of his power, his purpose and his love. We do well to heed the warnings given to the people of Israel on their journey to the promised land, as they too must have looked up into the sky: 'When you look up to the heavens and see the sun, the moon, and the stars, all the host of heaven, do not be led astray and bow down to them and serve them, things that the Lord your God has allotted to all the peoples everywhere under heaven' (Deuteronomy 4:19). Rather, we must look as the psalmist did, in awe and wonder praising God:

> When I look at your heavens, the work of your fingers,
> the moon and the stars that you have established;
> what are human beings that you are mindful of them,
> mortals that you care for them?'
> (Psalm 8:3–4)

We may look back at ancient civilizations who worshipped the sun and moon, and feel superior with all our modern 'know how', but are we spiritually any closer to recognizing the hand of God around us and above us? For all our cleverness, our understanding, why is the pull of 'the stars' of horoscopes so strong, why are the signs of the zodiac felt to have such a vital contribution to make in our development? Raise the issue and what is the answer? 'It's only a bit of fun, no one really takes it seriously…'. Ah, but they do! And there is a growing interest and involvement in astrology. 'New age' beliefs have become respectable and desirable, and exert a strong influence in today's society. Look in any major bookshop for books on spirituality and what will you find? For every Bible or Christian book there will be a dozen on the occult, the stars, and paganism in one of its many forms. There is, I believe, a great longing for a spiritual centre to life, but if it is not perceived to be available within the Christian Church then people will respond to the attractive and seductive invitations of pseudo-religious communities and groups, drawn to the column inches on 'what the stars foretell' rather than to the living word of God, which reveals the divine purpose and plan for all creation, and the way made clear for us to follow and find it.

The psalmist all those years ago recognized the majesty of God, and the dignity he has afforded humanity. Perhaps we, as people of the 21st century, need to relearn that lesson, and share it with the new generation, before they are driven to look elsewhere for satisfaction.

Yet you have made them a little lower than God,
and crowned them with glory and honour.
You have given them dominion over the works of your hands;
you have put all things under their feet...
O Lord our Sovereign,
how majestic is your name in all the earth.
PSALM 8:5–6, 9

Lord God, as I look into the sky I see your majesty, your beauty, your power. I see the sun, moon, stars, your creation, so far away in time and space, and yet visible to my eyes, touching my mind, my spirit, my soul, by the greatness of your glory.

What am I, puny creature here, living out my few short years, child of the earth, so vulnerable, so weak, so restricted? I long to touch the stars, to be warmed by the sun, enlightened by the moon; but the space between us is too great, the time too far, and I am so small and insignificant. Yet, wonder of wonders, you have reached down to me, touched me, held me by the power of your love made visible in human form—your Son, Jesus Christ. You come to me, you have searched me out, and enfolded me into your heart, your very being. I am your child, I have a dignity, a future. You raise me to the place I could never reach myself, you keep me safe for all eternity, O Lord, my God, my Saviour, my all.

You are my God, and I will give thanks to you;
you are my God, I will extol you.
O give thanks to the Lord, for he is good,
for his steadfast love endures for ever.
PSALM 118:28–29

Chapter 34

IS THERE STILL TIME?

Romantics may sigh, cynics sneer, philosophers debate, economists analyse, and politicians make of it what they will; but there is no doubt that we were all affected by crossing the divide that marked the end of the second millennium and the beginning of the third. We all jumped (or were we pushed?) into a new dimension of time. Many would say, 'What difference did a change in the date make? After all, not all the world dates time in the same way.' But it was more than marking off life in a mathematical manner, it was a staging-post which forced us to think about the purpose of our lives, the fundamental questions: 'Where did we come from? Why are we here? And where are we going?' Perhaps for most people they were only passing thoughts, but for some—and I include myself in this—it was a time to reflect, to adjust and to take to heart some of the lessons learned. I feel it has been an exciting time, and a great privilege to have been part of this 'once in a thousand years' point in history, to straddle not only two centuries but two millennia. After all, none of us will be around to do it again!

The BBC put it like this, 'The Millennium: reflect, celebrate, anticipate'. If we did that we gained something very special; and if we did not, there is still time! There were countless opportunities to be part of millennium projects, and many of these will enhance local communities for many years to come, such as playing fields, gardens, exhibitions, regeneration schemes, study centres, and the like. These projects helped to foster and support new initiatives and encouraged participants to go forward with confidence. Millennium grants have also enabled individuals to share their gifts and expertise, particularly within the arts, discovering latent talents, providing helping hands, and so aiding and developing the creative skills and interests which were there, but needed that 'seed corn' to bring them to birth and to grow.

The spiritual dimension was not neglected in all of this. One such project in Northumberland produced a six-feet by four-feet image of Christ made by a local artist, Ian Johnson, from 2800 individual pictures taken by residents of the village of Whalton. A millennium grant enabled the artist to give every villager a disposable camera to take pictures of their surroundings, of the countryside, landscapes, people, animals, every part of their daily life, and these were then all combined in the creation of 'Incarnation'—an image of the face of Christ, displayed at St Mary Magdalene's Church, Whalton. It was not just a picture but a parable, a reminder that as we look at Christ we see life, our own life, in all its many facets; and we are part of him, reflecting him by our active participation in showing the glory of God made flesh in 'Emmanuel—God with us'. Theology is brought to life, expressed in new and exciting forms of art and design.

One example I saw recently was constructed entirely from discarded rubbish found on a tip. Rubbish was redeemed through the loving hands of a craftsman, offered back in thanks and praise to God, creator of all things, who at the beginning saw everything he had made and pronounced it 'very good'. It is a far cry from the creation to our life today, but God is eternal, his truth remains throughout all time, ours included, revealed afresh in every generation, in each person who would know the truth. How we then express truth and make it relevant and attractive is by coming to the still source of all truth, letting go of our time-based existence and giving ourselves wholly and unreservedly into the enfolding, revealing hands of God. We can re-echo that prayer of John Greenleaf Whittier:

> Breathe through the heats of our desire,
> Thy coolness and thy balm.
> Let sense be dumb, let flesh retire;
> Speak through the earthquake, wind and fire,
> O still small voice of calm.

Only then will we realize our true value, and the value of every other human being, and every part of creation. We are not rubbish, disposable, useless, voiceless and powerless, even though in our 'throw-away' society of today it may often seem so. We are made in the image of God, and he has given us a dignity, a beauty, with our own unique contribution to make to life. We are part of the incarnation, here and now. We are part of Christ's body, active and alive, part of his hands, his heart, his voice, his feet; and he needs to be seen and experienced through us, so that we are, as Mother Teresa expressed it, 'something beautiful for God'.

Some advice I saw a while ago in a legal comment column said this: 'To get the true picture, always read the small print.' It reminds me of that picture of Christ made up of 2800 photographs, each one having its part in the whole. The global face of Christ is made up of millions, and is being added to every second—something well worth reminding ourselves of when we are told the Church is dying out, and failing in its task.

At the beginning of this book I described it as 'a series of snapshots, set in the frame of God's word'. Inevitably, these have been my own personal snapshots, coloured by my life and experiences; but I hope that through them you have been able to see beyond what I have seen and recorded to a wider, clearer picture, and to see where you are, and more importantly, where God is for you—a vision which will urge you to go on into the future, wherever it may take you. It is an invitation to discover the abundant life, which is God's gift to you, and to live it.

The writer Jolan Chang put it like this: 'Most of us are like owners of a precious Stradivarius violin that we have never learned to play' (*Reader's Digest*) We have each been given a wonderful life, with so much potential and promise, but like any instrument it is useless unless used, trained, enjoyed, disciplined, explored to the full. We are designed to express the glory of God, to draw others into that experience too; but we have to take up the bow and start learning to play. There is still time—all the time God has given us, all the world to express it in, and all eternity still before us. It is for us to discover the joy of the promise fulfilled, now.

Hear, O Lord, when I cry aloud,
be gracious to me and answer me.
'Come,' my heart says, 'seek his face!'
Your face, Lord, do I seek.
Do not hide your face from me.

PSALM 27:7–9

Father, I place into your hands now all my memories of the past;
all the way you have brought me, sustained and guided me;
all your many gifts and mercies so freely showered upon me.
I place into your hands this day, knowing that whatever happens,
you are with me, and will give me grace and strength for all it contains.
I place into your hands the future, confident and unafraid,
for you are there already. I have no need to fear
because I trust you to take me safely through.
I place myself, my past, my present and my future into your hands
for all eternity, in faith, and with love,
in the name of Jesus Christ, my Lord and my Saviour.

Nevertheless, I am continually with you;
you hold my right hand.
You guide me with your counsel,
and afterwards you will receive me with honour.

PSALM 73:23–24

Thanks be to God!

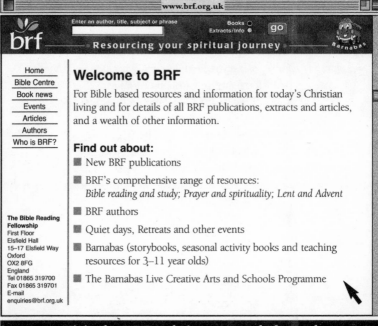

www.brf.org.uk

Enter an author, title, subject or phrase

Books ○
Extracts/Info ●

go

brf
Resourcing your spiritual journey

Home
Bible Centre
Book news
Events
Articles
Authors
Who is BRF?

The Bible Reading
Fellowship
First Floor
Elsfield Hall
15–17 Elsfield Way
Oxford
OX2 8FG
England
Tel 01865 319700
Fax 01865 319701
E-mail
enquiries@brf.org.uk

Welcome to BRF

For Bible based resources and information for today's Christian living and for details of all BRF publications, extracts and articles, and a wealth of other information.

Find out about:

- New BRF publications
- BRF's comprehensive range of resources:
  Bible reading and study; Prayer and spirituality; Lent and Advent
- BRF authors
- Quiet days, Retreats and other events
- Barnabas (storybooks, seasonal activity books and teaching resources for 3–11 year olds)
- The Barnabas Live Creative Arts and Schools Programme

Visit the BRF website at www.brf.org.uk

BRF is a Registered Charity